Called to Be HOLY

Rick Melick

LifeWay Press
Nashville, Tennessee

ISBN 0-6330-0370-0
Dewey Decimal Classification: 234.8
Subject Heading: SANCTIFICATION

This book is text for course CG-0656 in the subject area
Baptist Doctrine in the Christian Growth Study Plan.

Unless otherwise noted, Scripture quotations are from the Holy Bible,
New International Version, copyright © 1973, 1978, 1984
by International Bible Society.

Scripture quotations marked KJV are from the *King James Version.*

To order additional copies of this resource: WRITE LifeWay Church Resources
Customer Service, 127 Ninth Avenue, North; Nashville, TN 37234-0113;
FAX (615) 251-5933; PHONE 1-800-458-2772;
EMAIL *customerservice@lifeway.com;*
order ONLINE at *www.lifeway.com;* or visit the LifeWay Christian Store serving you.

Printed in the United States of America

LifeWay Press
127 Ninth Avenue, North
Nashville, Tennessee 37234-0151

*As God works through us, we will help people and churches
know Jesus Christ and seek His kingdom by providing biblical solutions
that spiritually transform individuals and cultures.*

CONTENTS

ABOUT THE AUTHOR

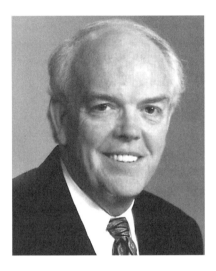

D r. Richard Melick currently serves as Provost and New Testament Professor at Golden Gate Baptist Theological Seminary. He is married to Shera who is a professor of Christian Education, also at the seminary. They have three children, Richard, Kristi, and Karen and four wonderful grandchildren.

Prior to serving at Golden Gate Seminary, Dr. Melick was president of the Criswell Center for Biblical Studies in Dallas. He has served at six other educational institutions during his teaching ministry and currently maintains a position of Visiting Professor at the Evangelische Theologische Faculteit in Heverlee, Belgium.

A former pastor of two churches and numerous interim pastorates, Dr. Melick is a recognized author. He serves as consulting editor for the *New American Commentary*. He is author of the series' volume on Philippians, Colossians, and Philemon and served as co-editor and contributor to *Authority and Interpretation: A Baptist Perspective*.

PREFACE

C alled to Be Holy, the 2002 Doctrine Study for the Southern Baptist Convention, surveys an important biblical theme. Holiness begins with God Himself—the model for all holiness. God's holiness never changes; it undergirds all of life for believers and unbelievers alike. Christians are called to be like God—to be holy. We learn what holiness means by focusing on Jesus Christ. He became flesh, in part, to show us how to live as we ought.

This year's study follows the study on God's *Amazing Grace*, providing a normal progression. No one can be holy without understanding God's grace. Paul said,

> *For the grace of God that brings salvation has appeared to all men. It teaches us to say "No" to ungodliness and worldly passions, and to live self-controlled, upright and godly lives in this present age, while we wait for the blessed hope— the glorious appearing of our great God and Savior, Jesus Christ, who gave himself for us to redeem us from all wickedness and to purify for himself a people that are his very own, eager to do what is good (Titus 2:11-14).*

God's grace enables Him to forgive our past, and His grace mysteriously enables us to overcome sin in our Christian lives. In relating to us by grace, He changes us into the holy character that He desires.

Christians must continually determine how best to represent Christ. Our lives stand as lights to a dark world, pointing people to God's standard that is the measure of the stature of Jesus Christ. The world influences us so that we have great difficulty keeping our spiritual equilibrium. So, unfortunately, the church sometimes looks more like the world than the world does.

The study has a twofold purpose: to present the doctrine of holiness in a readable and understandable way and to encourage the reader to pursue holiness personally. I have tried to organize the book in a useful and readable way. The text offers simple but important steps for attaining holiness. I have not unnecessarily included Greek and Hebrew words and technical exegesis. However, I have included many Scripture references to support the points I make. Chapters are divided into sections that, if understood and applied, provide a framework for understanding personal transformation. Since holiness is about transformation, I pray the book will challenge each reader's life as well as enlarge the mind.

I am grateful to those who encouraged me in this project. Don Atkinson, experienced editor of this series, graciously invited me to write and provided expert help along the way. Lena Finnan, my Administrative Assistant, read the manuscript and prepared it for publication. Her technical skills and godly insights have been a constant encouragement. Kristi Ent, my daughter, also read the manuscript and offered valuable suggestions as well as loving support. Dr. Bill Crews, President of Golden Gate Baptist Theological Seminary, encouraged me to accept the assignment suggesting this would be a worthy expenditure of time. I appreciate his friendship and continuing support. My colleagues at Golden Gate Baptist Theological Seminary constantly befriend, encourage, enrich, and challenge me in the things of God and His Kingdom.

I am indebted to what I have learned from my family through the years. Shera, my wife of 32 years, has lived in such a way that I am constantly challenged by her holy character, enriched by her companionship, and encouraged by her constant love. My three children and their spouses, Rick and Joy, Kristi and Michael, Karen and Darren, have enriched my life by their lives, their love for our Lord, and their faithfulness in responding to God's call for them to enter the ministry. Watching them I have seen holiness displayed in the uniqueness of wonderful individuality. Last, my four young grandchildren, Richard and Nathan, and Anna and Michael David, constantly remind me of the good things of life and challenge me to better living with their profound but simple faith in Christ. This book is dedicated to all of them.

During the writing process, I have had two constant prayers. With an increasing longing to be more like Jesus Christ, I have prayed that in some way I, too, will display His holy character. I've also prayed that the truths here will encourage others to be like Jesus Christ as well. In short, my hope is what has been my constant prayer for 35 years. The apostle Paul prayed it first for the church at Philippi: "And this is my prayer: that your love may abound more and more in knowledge and depth of insight, so that you may be able to discern what is best and may be pure and blameless until the day of Christ, filled with the fruit of righteousness that comes through Jesus Christ—to the glory and praise of God" (Phil. 1:9-11).

To my wife, Shera,
and my children,
Rick and Joy Melick, Kristi and Michael Ent,
and Karen and Darren Draeger
who share the quest for holiness,
and to my grandchildren,
Richard and Nathan Melick
and Anna and Michael David Ent,
whose young hearts are already sensitive to the Lord

Defining Holiness

CHAPTER 1
HOLINESS—GOOD FOR ALL OF US

Holiness, holiness, is what I long for
Holiness is what I need
Holiness, holiness is what
You want from me.[1]

The catchy tune and simple song grab our attention, and we easily join in the musical prayer. The song should express everyone's desire. All should long for holiness, righteousness, and faithfulness. If we really long for holiness, we have changed from self-centeredness to God's will. Nothing so describes the life of a Christian as the desire to be holy.

ATTITUDES TOWARD HOLINESS

Holiness has seldom been popular. Being holy means that people accept a different lifestyle from the norms of society. Many think of holy people as bizarre and eccentric. Holiness is something reserved for a select few called to be holy men, shamans, prophets, or priests. Through the centuries many have hoped others would be holy for them, assuming that priests, monks, nuns, and preachers should be holy since that is God's call on their lives.

The average person seems to have trouble keeping up with the demands of life and adding the burden of holiness only increases frustration. Increasingly, society considers religious people as its major problem rather than the solution to its ills. After all, most religions stand against many accepted social values such as following passions and the pursuit of wealth and pleasure as the ultimate goal. For many, holiness applies to those whose dress is out of date, who refuse to enjoy modern entertainment, and who decry others who do.

These anti-Christian attitudes have been encouraged by two trends. The first is increased secularism. Church attendance has decreased, and most religions report fewer followers. The media encourages pleasure and ego satisfaction as the highest good. They entice people away from theistic roots and traditional values. Secularism focuses on the immediate and erodes the commitments of the most devout.

The second major trend is the confusion of good and evil. The rise of witchcraft, satanism, naturalistic religions and new age beliefs undermines Christian faith. It is not uncommon today to hear people advocate sexual promiscuity, extramarital affairs, unethical behavior, and deceit. There is a direct attack against God and His Word. The undertow of modern life pulls all of us toward the sea of relativism.

The undertow of modern life pulls all of us toward the sea of relativism.

Generations of Christians have fought their battles against the inroads of secularism. Since the early 1900s, many church leaders preached the need for Christians to live separate lives. The most extreme separatists decried the ills of almost everything their contemporaries embraced. It was normal to hear the evils of "dancing, drinking, movies, pool halls, rock music, mixed swimming," and the list could go on. They said genuine Christians could not associate with people who did not live by these same convictions.

These people had high ideals, but often they reduced Christian holiness to lists of do's and don'ts. Many of the issues on their lists could not be found in the Bible, but lists provide a safe retreat from life. Ostensibly they provided clear-cut answers to the questions of godliness. But while these people had legitimate concerns, they often misunderstood true biblical motivations for godliness. Many of them also misapplied Scripture to situations it never intended to address. At conversion God delivers us from the Old

Testament Laws and regulations. He does not expect Christians to trade the Old Testament Law from which they are delivered for another "Christian law" to measure our spiritual successes. God desires a more relational life for His people.

The "separationists" had a basically negative view of the world. While acknowledging the world as God's handiwork, they also saw it as the home of Satan and evil. For many, culture was incurably evil. The only way to develop holiness was to flee culture. God's way was always different from the world's—and to be Christian meant to be different.

This approach to Christian living brought strong reactions. The last two generations in America asked serious questions about virtually everything. In the sixties and seventies rebellion was in the air. People rebelled against established government, religion, social mores, family, and, most of all, rules. Christians also asked questions. Why were the do's and don'ts advocated by past generations so binding? Does God really expect His people to be horribly "out of step" as so many had advocated? Was there any real virtue in being "odd for God"? That type of "holiness" often repelled non-Christians. There was hardly anything that would attract them to the faith as long as "separation" was the watchword. At the same time, groups like the "Jesus Freaks" often had a dynamic, faith which did not always accept the patterns of the established church.

God promises fulfillment, satisfaction of our deepest desires, and the joy that everyone seeks.

Some of the most effective communicators of the gospel changed the tone of their preaching to a more positive message than "being different from the world." Their messages usually focused on real life. They understood that God promises fulfillment, satisfaction of our deepest desires, and the joy that everyone seeks. Christianity was often explained in psychological or relational terms, rather than the more traditional theological ones. There was less emphasis on "being different" and more stress on "being fulfilled."

This alternative view was more positive. While recognizing the world's evils, these Christians accepted the purity of what God created. Was it necessary to flee from everything? Were all people to be avoided simply because they were not Christians? Were all activities, events, foods, and pleasures wrong simply because they were enjoyable? Did God really expect us to repudiate what He had made? After all, He entrusted creation to human beings, and surely He expects us to appreciate it.

This was a new way of looking at the Christian life that tended to accept people for their Christian commitment without dividing over minor issues. It brought serious challenges to the previous theology of holiness.

These tensions were not new. A reading of history reveals a deep concern for responsible Christian living. Early Christian thinkers devoted countless hours to the task of developing proper convictions about life and holiness. Some resorted to external "lists" and "activity-oriented approaches," while others were more inner and personal. The fact is Christians differ and they always have.

How are we to find our way to the joy and freedom of Christ? The only solid foundation is God revealed in His Word. Spiritual equilibrium comes from embracing what does not change and applying that to changing life situations.

Spiritual equilibrium comes from embracing what does not change and applying that to changing life situations.

PERSONAL LEARNING ACTIVITY

The author writes that we find joy and freedom of Christ in God's Word. List some ways you daily pattern your life after God's Word.

_____

_____

CALLED TO BE HOLY

There are many approaches to holiness. Some come directly from human experiences, some from contemporary philosophy or psychology, and some from theology. There are also different attitudes about the Bible's application to contemporary thinking on personal transformation. One approach begins with prevailing philosophies, psychologies, or theologies and quotes Bible verses to prove that so-called "secular" ideas may really be "biblical." This often amounts to "baptizing" non-Christian ideas and seeking to demonstrate biblical support by proof-texting. The other approach begins with Scripture, seeking to systematize its teachings apart from the prevailing theories of the secular world. Adherents of this approach may or may not use contemporary cultural language to connect the Bible and secular theories. Sometimes advocates of this approach believe that others corrupt the faith by using "secular" language.

Biblical integrity goes far deeper than using theological words to express concepts.

Either approach can be misguided. Using the language of a prevailing culture (English, for example) to explain Christian living may reveal a lack of serious understanding of Scripture and theology. In its worst form it may be nothing more than secular thinking expressed through biblical language. Biblical integrity goes far deeper than using theological words to express concepts. Besides, contemporary language sometimes expresses biblical truths quite adequately and clearly. In its worst form, expressing biblical theology with non-biblical language may be faddish or trendy and fail to have biblical depth.

The practical difference between the two became apparent to me many years ago. I team-taught a college Sunday School class with one of the local professors of psychology at the university. From all I observed he was a model Christian. One Sunday he introduced the lesson with this question: "Is man good or bad?" The 175 college students in the room did not know how to answer his question. He tried to promote thought and discussion by posing the question with more theological relevance: "What does the

Bible say?" "The Bible says man is bad!" So he wrote *Bible* and *bad* on one end of the chalk board. "What does psychology say?" "Psychology says man is good!" He wrote *psychology* and *good* on the other end of the board. Suddenly a light dawned in his thinking. He realized he had identified one of the most difficult of all issues–the relationship between Scripture and modern thought. Quickly he responded, "Well, we cannot get into that!" and moved on with his lesson.

Actually the dichotomy between the two was not totally accurate. The Bible does not say human beings are "bad" as many commonly understand the word. It does say everyone is sinful and that "being bad" comes from sinfulness. On the other hand, not all psychologists would say people are "good." Some recognize the innate tendency to sin. Nevertheless, the differences between the Bible and many psychological theories exist. Because of this, Christians should develop solid biblical principles of holiness.

In this study, we will provide an overview of what God says about holiness in the Scriptures. We will also take a functional approach that assumes the practical nature of holiness. The goal is to find a balance between the theology of holiness and the biblical teaching of how to become holy. Holiness requires changes in life. Without understanding this, holiness does not relate to our lives.

Holiness requires changes in life.

PERSONAL LEARNING ACTIVITY

Holiness requires life change. Are there specific areas in your life that require change? List them below, and ask God to help you through His Spirit to address these areas of change.

———————————————————————

———————————————————————

Holiness is a controversial subject. My goal is to provide information leading to serious reflection, informed discussion, and better Christian living. As you read, please evaluate the material prayerfully, determining whether the goal has been accomplished and asking God to reward the effort with a closer likeness to Christ.

Because of the practical concerns, this book is divided into three sections. In section 1, I attempt to define *holiness*, to explore the biblical definitions, and to present the various major evangelical theologies of sanctification. In section 2, I consider the process of life transformation. With a focus on practical, biblical teaching, it presents the process of how to become holy. Finally, in section 3, I focus on achieving the goal of complete holiness. In chapter 6, you will find suggested helps and a brief description of what complete holiness will be like.

GOD EXPECTS HOLINESS

God expects people to be holy.

God expects people to be holy. The absolute bedrock of Christian living is holiness. This expectation is based on His holy nature. Most frequently the Bible describes God as holy, and the biblical presentation of God's holiness is positive rather than negative. God's desire for us is for our own good. Christian living involves holiness because Christians should be like God Himself.

GOD IS HOLY

Perhaps the most fundamental principle of the universe is God's holiness. His holiness explains how He can reign in righteousness unaffected by the evil that influences us. When the power of God is manifest, it is often associated with His holiness. God's intervention into the affairs of life is always redemptive or corrective with moral implications properly associated with holiness. Because He is holy, He always wills what is right. Therefore, the relationship between God and people is based on holiness.

14

God is holy! God's holiness permeates both the Old and New Testaments. In the Old Testament the Hebrew word translated *holy* is *qadosh*. It means "apartness or sacredness." It properly describes God but can also be used of things or places dedicated to God. In this sense the word describes the temple, refers to the biblically commanded sacrifices, and characterizes the furniture of the temple as well. The Bible makes clear that when things belong to God, they are set apart to honor Him. They are holy. Sometimes the adjective form of the word occurs. The adjective identifies the power and majesty of God as being separate or apart. God is separate from humans as well. When we think of God's holiness, the most common thought is how different He is from us. He is above human frailty, impurity, and sin.

GOD EXPECTS US TO BE HOLY

God's holiness calls for a human holiness. The Old Testament contains many examples of God delighting in His relationships with holy people. The Bible teaches that no one can have a relationship with God without holiness. The story of redemption is the story of holiness lost and gained.

God created us to be holy. The creation accounts reveal that we are made "in his own image" (Gen. 1:27). Although theologians debate the precise meaning of the *imagio dei*–the image of God in us–one aspect of it is clear: human beings have moral capacity. We have the ability to choose right and wrong. In the garden of Eden, Adam and Eve had not experienced good or evil, yet they had the capacity to experience both. He created human beings in such a way that we can choose the kind of life we wish to live.

God created man in his own image, in the image of God he created him; male and female he created them.
Genesis 1:27

The first choice made in recorded history was a choice by Adam and Eve against God. The origins of all our problems lie in that first decision. It was a decision that introduced sin into the world, tainting every subsequent decision any person would make. The decision meant that the world seems to revolve around my life and your life, and me and you, rather than God and His will.

The reality of human sin provides the key to understanding the remainder of the Bible. God created us to have an intimate relationship with Him. Since we are created that way, the only way to achieve ultimate personal fulfillment is to live as God intends. Yet sin distorts everything about us so that we cannot understand God's ways.

The only way to achieve ultimate personal fulfillment is to live as God intends.

Immediately after the fall into sin, God began to explain redemption. In Genesis 3:15 God promised a Savior from the descendants of Eve. This Messiah, Jesus, would defeat Satan. In His victory sin would also be defeated, allowing people who trust Jesus to regain the holiness lost by the original fall into sin. Theologians differ about how closely sanctification and conversion should be linked. All agree, however, that there is no possibility of personal holiness without a genuine knowledge of Jesus Christ, the Messiah. Genuine knowledge involves the mind and the heart. The mind accepts the truths about Jesus which must be understood correctly for salvation. The heart embraces Jesus in an all-encompassing trusting relationship.

In the final analysis, the Bible is about being holy. The Bible teaches us to become what God wills for us. Today we often use different terminology to explain what that means. Today, it is common to hear terms like *self-actualization, self-fulfillment, happiness,* and *contentment.* The list could go on. Each word communicates distinctly to human experience, but these descriptive phrases have something in common. All of them basically explain what God means in using the term *holiness.* We as humans approach life from a self-centered and fragmented perspective. We talk about the need for personal satisfaction. The Bible approaches life holistically from God's perspective. The Bible explains that such things as personal satisfaction, fulfillment, and contentment come as by-products of holiness—but not before or without it. The more

we are holy, the more we are satisfied because personal fulfillment comes from being holy like God.

OLD TESTAMENT TEACHING

In the Old Testament God reveals His plan to redeem people from sin. God presents His plan in direct teaching and
with pictures He provided for our understanding. While
the central theme of the Old Testament is redemption,
much of the history of the Old Testament describes the
development of the nation Israel. The reason for this occurs
in Genesis 3:15. The passage describes the time when God
first approached Adam and Eve after their sin. In that verse
He predicted the course of human history. History involves
a battle in which Satan will bruise the heel of God's
Redeemer, but God's Redeemer will crush the head of
Satan. The Redeemer will be human, the offspring of Eve.
While it often seems that history is haphazard, the Bible
explains that God works through it all.

I will put enmity between you and the woman and between your offspring and hers; he will crush your head, and you will strike his heel.
Genesis 3:15

History is intertwined with theology. God chose the nation
Israel to be the vehicle of His redemption. The leaders of the
young nation responded to God's call. They knew that God
would use them and their offspring to bless the world with
the Messiah. As God's special agents, they also realized their
high responsibility to reveal the true God to the world. They
were to be holy as God is holy.

DIRECT TEACHINGS OF THE OLD TESTAMENT

The Old Testament clearly and directly expresses God's call
to holiness. After God delivered the nation from Egypt and
gave them a government through Moses and the Ten Commandments, He inspired Moses to write the first five books
of the Bible. One of those books is Leviticus.

The theme of Leviticus is holiness. In the entire Old Testament, the word *holiness* occurs 360 times in 331 verses. This
means that Leviticus contains 20 percent of the uses of the

word, a disproportionate number considering there are 39 books of the Old Testament. The phrase, "Be holy for I am holy" (11:44) is generally considered the theme of Leviticus, even though it occurs only one time in the book and only once in the entire Old Testament. It succinctly explains God's will for His people, and it provides the rationale for the entire message of Leviticus. As a microcosm of the Old Testament teaching, Leviticus clearly teaches that God is holy and that His people must strive for holiness as well.

God alone is holy and His holiness stands as one of the primary characteristics of Israel's God.

Often God introduced Himself as the *Holy One*. The title occurs 50 times in 48 different verses of the Old Testament. The self-description implies that God alone is holy and that His holiness stands as one of the primary characteristics of Israel's God. Thus, Israel is to appreciate, worship, and emulate God's holiness.

OLD TESTAMENT PICTURES

The Old Testament clarifies the implications of God's holiness by describing how people are to relate to their holy God. These implications occur especially in the places where God disclosed the standards of holiness for those who would serve and worship Him.

Again, the Book of Leviticus serves as the focus of this discussion. It is an instruction book for worship practices. Three kinds of instruction provided information for God's people of that day. They were the standards for those who serve God, the standards for the sacrificial animals, and the standards of the sacrificial rituals. These standards, which are recounted in Leviticus, not only help us to picture God's holiness but also reinforce the concept of holiness.

Standards for those who serve God. Sometimes people assume God is unfair, especially to those who do not match up to His standards. This is hardly the case. The fact is that God instructed His people in accord with His nature. His holy nature demands the best.

18

The standards may be noticed in the qualifications for the priesthood. By law the priesthood was limited to those of the family of Levi, the Levites. Since the Levites did not receive an inheritance of land like the other tribes, their inheritance was the priesthood (see Deut. 10:8-9). Not all Levites actually served as priests, however. Aaron and his sons were anointed with oil as priests, and they wore the special clothing of the priesthood (see Ex. 28–29). Additionally, the families of Eli (see 1 Sam. 14:3), Zadok (see Ezek. 40:46), and Amaziah (see Amos 7:10-17) were priests.

There were other restrictions besides family line. A priest could not serve if he had a physical defect (see Lev. 21:16-24). There were marriage restrictions which stated they could marry only a virgin of Israel and were forbidden marriage with a divorcee, prostitute, proselyte, or widow (see Lev. 21:7-9,13-15). Further, they could not officiate in the sacrificial rituals if they were ritualistically impure or were under the influence of alcohol. They could not visit a cemetery nor could they be around the dead unless they were of the immediate family (see Lev. 21:1-3).

The higher restrictions placed on the priests were because of their high calling. They were expected to preserve the holiness of the tabernacle, and they represented God to the people. The priests also officiated in the rituals that enabled the people to draw near to God. The high standards prerequisite for the priesthood served to remind the people of the necessity of holiness in order to have fellowship with God. The standards disqualified some from serving, but to lower the standard would cause an errant picture of God.

Priests were expected to preserve the holiness of the tabernacle, and they represented God to the people.

Standards for the sacrificial animals. The requirements were high. The most basic requirement was that the sacrifice had to be from "clean animals and clean birds" (Gen. 8:20). People could sacrifice cattle, goats, sheep, doves, or pigeons (see Gen. 15:9), but camels and donkeys were forbidden, even though they were readily available.

More specific regulations were to be enforced. Male animals were preferred over females (see Lev. 1:3). Older animals, at least three years old, were preferred over the young (see 1 Sam. 1:24), and the sacrificial animals were to be as physically perfect as possible (see Lev. 1:3; 3:1). This gave rise to the need for the priests to examine the animals to guarantee that they fulfilled these requirements.

Holiness is a prerequisite for worship, for fellowship with God, and for bringing the sacrifices.

These requirements pictured God as holy. They also reminded the people that holiness is a prerequisite for worship, for fellowship with God, and for bringing the sacrifices. Israel knew that they were to bring the best for God. Everything about the sacrificial system spoke against the idea that just anything would do for God.

Standards of the sacrificial rituals. Generally, there were six steps in the process of the sacrifices. While they differed somewhat depending on the specific nature of the sacrifice, the pattern is instructive.

The steps are as follows: *step one*–the worshiper brought the sacrifice to the altar symbolic of the desire to draw near to God; *step two*–the worshiper laid his hand, or hands, on the sacrificial animal. This symbolic act reminded the sacrificer of the intimate connection between the animal to be sacrificed and the one who offered it. The animal represented the person offering it. With hands on the animal, the worshiper confessed his sins if it were a sin offering. In confession the worshiper acknowledged that sin must be taken seriously, and the death of the animal symbolically brought forgiveness; *step three*–in the case of animal sacrifices, the worshiper slaughtered the animal personally. The personal aspect of this allowed the individual to assume responsibility for the sin that caused the animal's death; *step four*–the priest took the blood from the animal and carefully sprinkled it on the altar in a way that symbolized cleansing;. *step five*–most sacrifices included burning parts of the animal. This represented offering God both the inside and outside of the animal; *step six*–much of the meat of the offering was eaten. Sometimes the worshiper ate with the priests, but most often the priests and their families shared the meat.

This general overview of the sacrificial system provides insight into the Holy God's expectations. Since people are unholy, the ritualistic and symbolic cleansing reminded the people of the seriousness of their sin. The sacrifice also taught them that it was necessary to offer a perfect life to atone for sin. When the worshiper personally participated in the ritual, there was a sense of personal need. Worshipers accepted responsibility for their sins and for bringing their best to God. Nothing less would do.

Worshipers accepted responsibility for their sins and for bringing their best to God. Nothing less would do.

The last book of the Old Testament also calls the people to holiness. Malachi warned the people of bringing sick and weak animals for sacrifice (see Mal. 1:8-14). He decried the sinful living of the priests (see Mal. 2:1-9) and deplored the generally unholy way people cared for their land.

The Old Testament consistently develops several themes:
* God is holy. Holiness is essential to His character.
* People are sinful and therefore unholy. Sin separates us from God and makes it impossible to have a relationship with God on our own. God's holiness means that He can have fellowship only with those who share His holiness. God's holiness is also the basis of His justice.
* It is possible to relate to God through the intervention of a substitute who gave up His life to make this relationship possible. The animal sacrifices pictured One who could die and through His death provide life. Prophetically, they pictured God's provision of salvation through Jesus Christ.

New Testament Teaching

Like the Old Testament, the New Testament develops the concept of holiness. Once again there are direct statements, and there are images that call us to holiness.

DIRECT TEACHINGS OF THE NEW TESTAMENT

In the New Testament three word groups refer to the idea of being holy. The most commonly used contains the word *hagios* which is the most frequent and the most important for our study.[2] Normally translators translate the noun as "holy," or "sacred." The other most common words in the group are translated as "make holy, consecrate, sanctify," and "holiness, consecration, sanctification."[3]

The New Testament uses these words in a slightly different way from the Old Testament. For example, the words describe God much less frequently. Also, the words are not used primarily in the temple and sacrificial arenas. Instead, they are more often associated with people. This follows a common fulfillment motif in the Old Testament that the temple and sacrifices pointed to a coming Messiah.

These words are used in two important ways to directly influence the New Testament concept of holiness. First, all persons of the Trinity are called holy. The following references help clarify the issue. God the Father has a holy name, an exact equivalent to calling His person holy (see Luke 1:49). God the Son, Jesus, is called holy in multiple places by demons (see Mark 1:24), by Peter in his confession of Jesus' death (see John 6:69), and by Peter in his public preaching (see Acts 4:27). God the Spirit has the attribute of holiness associated with Him in His name. He is most often called the Holy Spirit. Each person of the Trinity is to be set apart, honored, and worshiped as holy.

Each person of the Trinity is to be set apart, honored, and worshiped as holy.

The second point of difference with the Old Testament is the fact that the holiness words identify different people as holy. While the Old Testament restricted the primary use to priests and others who serviced the temple, the New Testament applies it to all of the saints.

The New Testament also indicates that the entire Trinity shapes us toward holiness. Bible students recognize the distinctive work of each person of the Trinity in our salvation. God the Father chooses, God the Son accomplishes salvation, and God the Holy Spirit applies it to our lives so that we come to Christ. Each person of the Trinity has a unique task in accomplishing God's plan. Even so, the New Testament identifies each person of the Trinity with our holiness. Paul prayed for the Thessalonians that God the Father would "sanctify you through and through" (1 Thess. 5:23), having said earlier that sanctification was "God's will" for them (4:3). Speaking to the Corinthians Paul explained that because of God the Father's working, "You are in Christ Jesus, who has become for us wisdom from God–that is, our righteousness, holiness and redemption" (1 Cor. 1:30).

At conversion Jesus is our sanctification. Sanctification is also a joint working of the Son and the Holy Spirit. Contrasting the Christian lifestyle with that of unbelievers, Paul reminded them "you were washed, you were sanctified, you were justified in the name of the Lord Jesus Christ and by the Spirit of our God" (1 Cor. 6:11). Finally, sanctification can be described as the work of the Holy Spirit both in bringing us to salvation (see 1 Pet. 1:1-2) and in working God's purity in us (see 1 Thess. 4:7-8).

Sanctification can be described as a work of the Holy Spirit both in bringing us to salvation and in working God's purity in us.

New Testament Pictures

The New Testament encourages holiness by the use of metaphors describing the identity of believers. In the Old Testament, holiness was centered in the temple. The temple was dedicated to God, the sacrifices had to be holy, and the priests and Levites had a higher responsibility to live holy lives. In the New Testament, these three aspects of the temple and its activity are applied to Christians.

Christians are the new temple. We have the responsibility of displaying God's attributes. Jesus anticipated this in His ministry. When questioned about His authority for chasing money changers from the temple, He pointed to His own resurrection but implied a time when the temple would no longer be needed (see John 2:19-22). When the Samaritan woman questioned Jesus about the best place to worship, Jesus responded that the time had come when the place did not matter. With Jesus' arrival on earth, it was more important to know how to worship than where to worship. Those who "worship in spirit and truth" will truly worship the Father (John 4:21-24). Paul had this in mind when he encouraged the Corinthian Christians to holy living by explaining: "We are the temple of the living God. As God has said: 'I will live with them and walk among them, and I will be their God, and they will be my people'" (2 Cor. 6:16).

Christians are the new sacrifice. In Romans 12:1-2, Paul used terminology of the temple sacrificial system to explain how we are to relate to our holy God. We are to present our bodies to Him with the same care of ourselves that the Old Testament saint gave to selecting and offering a sacrificial animal. The sacrifices for sin to gain mercy in the Old Testament are replaced by our offering ourselves to God because of His mercy.

Christians are God's priests. The apostle Peter emphasized this to his readers who, being Jewish, understood the significance of the temple rituals. He explained that we Christians "are a chosen people, a royal priesthood, a holy nation, a people belonging to God" (1 Pet. 2:9). This verse originally applied to the nation Israel, but now referred to Christians as God's special representatives. Also earlier in this one passage, Peter used all three of the images we have discussed to remind Christians of our calling: "You also, like living stones, are being built into a spiritual house to be a holy priesthood, offering spiritual sacrifices acceptable to God through Jesus Christ" (v. 5). Equating believers to the sacred rituals of Israel serves to remind us of the high and holy calling of God on our lives.

The New Testament presents two major points regarding holiness. First, holiness is used in a way that identifies

I urge you, brothers, in view of God's mercy, to offer your bodies as living sacrifices, holy and pleasing to God—this is your spiritual act of worship. Do not conform any longer to the pattern of this world, but be transformed by the renewing of your mind. Then you will be able to test and approve what God's will is—his good, pleasing and perfect will.
Romans 12:1-2

whatever is holy as separate from the world. Second, holiness is used in a way that challenges believers to become holy, separate from the sinfulness of the world.

NEW TESTAMENT CLARIFICATION OF HOLINESS: TO BE LIKE JESUS

The New Testament teaches holiness in many of the same ways as the Old Testament. We observed that people were created in the image of God. The New Testament continues the theme both of the distortion of the image of God and the possibility of God's restoring His image in believers.

The most direct teaching on the fulfillment of the image of God in Christians occurs in Paul's Prison Epistles, Ephesians and Colossians. In Colossians, Paul spoke to the church about personal purity. Paul stated, "Do not lie to each other, since you have taken off your old self with its practices and have put on the new self, which is being renewed in knowledge in the image of its Creator" (Col. 3:9-10). The goal for the new person in Christ, "the new self," is to be "renewed in knowledge in the image of its Creator" (v. 10).

Jesus is consistently described in the New Testament as the Creator (see John 1:1-4; Heb. 1:1-3). In Colossians 1:16 Paul stated, "For by him all things were created: things in heaven and on earth, visible and invisible, whether thrones or powers or rulers or authorities; all things were created by him and for him." Jesus is the image of God. Paul taught this truth in Colossians 1:15: "He is the image of the invisible God, the firstborn over all creation." Further, Paul stated, "Here there is no Greek or Jew, circumcised or uncircumcised, barbarian, Scythian, slave or free, but Christ is all, and is in all" (3:11). Jesus brings all that God is to us.

The goal of holiness is to be like Jesus (see Rom. 8:29; 1 Cor. 15:49; 2 Cor. 3:18; Phil. 3:21).

For those God foreknew he also predestined to be conformed to the likeness of his Son.
Romans 8:29

25

Jesus is the One who makes God the Father visible and who brings the benefits of God to earth.

The New Testament makes the Old Testament teaching concrete, understandable, and manageable. Jesus is the image of God. The Epistle to the Hebrews expresses this unmistakenly. In Hebrews 1:3, Jesus is said to be "the radiance of God's glory and the exact representation of his being." Jesus is the One who makes God the Father visible and who brings the benefits of God to earth. Hebrews reveals that Jesus was exactly God; no one is like Him. If we can live like Him, we will have fulfilled God's expectations.

PERSONAL LEARNING ACTIVITY

The Bible says we are to "put off the old self." List ways you continue to be influenced by the old self.

_____

_____

List ways you are being made new in the attitude of your mind.

_____

_____

---

[1]Scott Underwood, "Holiness" from *15 Songs Proclaiming His Holiness*, Vineyard Music Group, 1998.

[2]The second word is *ieros,* which occurs very infrequently in the New Testament. It refers to what is consecrated by God's power. The word basically means something is intrinsically holy. It refers to the "holy Scriptures" (2 Tim. 3:15), and its neuter form refers almost always to the "holy place," the temple (Matt. 4:5), meaning Herod's temple. As might be expected, it occurs primarily in the Gospels with a literal meaning. The third word group is represented by the noun *osios.* This word occurs less than a dozen times in the New Testament, and is usually a quote from the Greek translation of the Old Testament, the Septuagint.

[3]Horst Seebass, "Holy, Consecrate, Sanctify, Saints, Devout," in *The New International Dictionary of New Testament Theology,* vol. 2, ed. Colin Brown (Grand Rapids, Mich.: Zondervan Publishing House, 1976), 223-38.

CHAPTER 2

THE MEANING OF HOLINESS

A man had received a ticket for speeding. When the judge asked how he pleaded, he started into a long, progressively louder monologue as to why he was not guilty. His defense was simple. "Your honor, I'm a holy man, and I cannot sin. I was not speeding." The people in the courtroom began to laugh, causing the man to give his defense all the louder. Finally to preserve order in the court, the judge stated, "Don't do it again, dismissed!" All the way out the door, the man shouted, "I'm a holy, righteous man, and I can't sin."

Many questions arise about what personal holiness actually means. In this chapter I hope to clarify some of the basic theological terminology as well as to explore briefly the major evangelical approaches to holy living. Holiness overlaps sanctification so that the words practically interchange. A biblical survey of the uses places the focus on being made holy at conversion and being made completely holy in glory. Nevertheless, there are times when the word *holiness* clearly conveys an ongoing sense of sanctification Many theologians make the words *holy* and *sanctification* synonymous. Throughout the book I use the two almost synonymously.

What does personal holiness actually mean?

THE DIMENSIONS OF HOLINESS

The Bible identifies different dimensions of holiness. From one perspective, sanctification occurs immediately at conversion. From another, it requires constant attention and progressively produces complete transformation. All believers feel a constant tendency toward sin and in reflective moments realize that throughout life we need to grow in personal holiness.

IMMEDIATE POSITIONAL HOLINESS

At conversion we are complete in Christ. At that time God guarantees us all the blessings eternal life brings. He views us through the "lens" of Jesus, so that each time He relates to us He recognizes our relationship to His Son. The relationship between the believer and Christ enables God to consider the experiences of Jesus as those of the believer.

At conversion God views us through the "lens" of Jesus Christ.

WE ARE FORGIVEN

The Bible teaches that at conversion we identify with Jesus' life and death. First, God places our sins on Jesus so that His death paid the price for our sin. We stand before God clean, as without sin, since through Jesus, God forgives our sins—past, present, and future. We have a right relationship with God. He always sees us as intimately associated to Jesus, and in Jesus' death, we, too, died. The apostle Paul described this in Romans: "Or don't you know that all of us who were baptized into Christ Jesus were baptized into his death? We were therefore buried with him through baptism into death in order that, just as Christ was raised from the dead through the glory of the Father, we too may live a new life. If we have been united with him like this in his death, we will certainly also be united with him in his resurrection" (6:3-5).

PERSONAL LEARNING ACTIVITY

In your words write a short paragraph on what it means to identify with Jesus' life and death.

_____

_____

_____

WE ARE MADE RIGHTEOUS

The second truth is that at conversion God considers Jesus' righteousness as ours. When God sees Jesus' life as ours, He treats us the same way He treats Jesus. From this perspective, He considers us as completely holy. Just as Jesus never sinned, so, in God's mind, we have never sinned. God can bless us with the good things of eternal life because He no longer sees our sins which He forgave in Jesus' death. And He no longer sees our failures since He sees us connected to Jesus' life.

Paul based this side of the truth on the life of David. Though David was a sinner, he experienced the blessings of a right relationship with God. Paul quoted Psalm 32:1-2 in Romans 4:

> *David says the same thing when he speaks of the blessedness of the man to whom God credits righteousness apart from works: "Blessed are they whose transgressions are forgiven, whose sins are covered. Blessed is the man whose sin the Lord will never count against him" (vv. 6-8).*

These complementary perspectives reveal a great truth about our salvation. From the moment of conversion God sees us as holy. We stand before Him completely holy, our sins forgiven and put away by God. The recognition of this truth allowed Paul to deal with the Corinthian church from the perspective of their relationship to God. The Corinthian church was the most problem-ridden and sinful church of the New Testament era, but Paul wrote, "To the church of God in Corinth, to those sanctified in Christ Jesus and called to be holy" (1 Cor. 1:2). Surely this church occupied more of the apostles' time and energy than any other church we know. Scholars generally conclude that Paul made at least three visits to Corinth to help establish and strengthen the church. Additionally, Paul wrote at least four letters to the church at Corinth. One preceded 1 Corinthians (see 1 Cor. 5:9, which refers to a previous letter). He wrote another

From the moment of conversion God sees us as holy.

between what we now know as 1 and 2 Corinthians. It was a harsh letter dealing with a matter of church discipline (see 2 Cor. 7:8, which is generally understood to refer to a letter after 1 Corinthians). Yet, he introduced his epistle to these believers by calling them "sanctified."

First Corinthians reveals anything but a holy people. The church was divided into parties. The church refused to take a stand against blatant and publicly acknowledged immorality. Relationships among Christians deteriorated to the point that believers actually sought legal action from the state to resolve issues between themselves and other members. They had theological problems with the exercise of spiritual gifts, questions about marriage, and divisions at the Lord's Supper as well as the accompanying Agape Feast. The church hardly seemed "sanctified."

Yet, Paul approached them confidently because of their relationship with Christ. They were in Christ. Therefore, they were sanctified. God saw them as His people, pure enough that He could relate to them as His own. No biblical text so clearly expresses the truth that at conversion God sees us differently. He no longer looks at us and sees the enormity of our sin. He sees us as completely holy because of the death and life of Jesus.

PERSONAL LEARNING ACTIVITY

The author says "He (God) sees us as completely holy because of the death and life of Jesus." Do you see yourself as holy?

How does Jesus' life and death make us holy?

The Letter to the Ephesians confirms the same truth. In praying for the church and hoping they would experience the magnificence of God's power, Paul said this "power is like the working of his mighty strength, which he exerted in Christ when he raised him from the dead and seated him at his right hand in the heavenly realms, far above all rule and authority, power and dominion, and every title that can be given, not only in the present age but also in the one to come" (1:19-21). Thus, Paul described their experience as related to the same power that raised Jesus from the dead.

In chapter 2 the same description fits the believer. There Paul stated: "But because of his great love for us, God, who is rich in mercy, made us alive with Christ even when we were dead in transgressions—it is by grace you have been saved. And God raised us up with Christ and seated us with him in the heavenly realms in Christ Jesus, in order that in the coming ages he might show the incomparable riches of his grace, expressed in his kindness to us in Christ Jesus" (vv. 4-7). Both Jesus and the believer are "raised" from the dead and "seated" in the heavenly realms. If the believer is already "seated" in the heavenly realms because of our identification with Christ, clearly God sees us and treats us as already holy.

Theologians often call this standing with God *positional* or *legal holiness*. Both terms attempt to express what is true about us but which is not fully realized in our experience. *Positional*, preferred by many, describes a situation different from what we normally think of ourselves. We would not see ourselves as holy. Yet God placed us in that "position" in Christ, and He views us there. *Legal*, preferred by others, recognizes a true condition based on the pronouncement of a judge. It comes from the use of the Pauline term *justification*. Justification means that God pronounces the believer just. It says nothing about our actual condition. In fact, believers are guilty and deserve punishment. But when the Judge, God, pronounces us just, that ruling prevails. Describing something as "legal" adequately conveys the

Justification means that God pronounces the believer just.

truth of God's perspective. The Judge can declare us just because of our identification with Christ.

At conversion something real happens. The believer is set apart for God. Yet more seems to happen when God sets us apart. We are changed. Our lives may not immediately display the completeness of character we hope we will have, but we have new desires and directions. Being set apart brings with it the desire to live in a manner consistent with being set apart by God.

Similarly, *positional holiness* means that God declares us holy. It has no reference as to how we live. It refers to what God says based on our identification with Christ. However, this positional holiness enables God to speak with us, to bring strength to us, to cause us to grow in Christian virtues, and to use us in His service.

Positional holiness means that God declares us holy.

The focus of this book is to put parameters on what holiness is for us. Chapters 3 through 5 describe what being set apart to God looks like. They discuss the intuitive changes at conversion that will be infleshed by each individual in various ways. The desire to fulfill the standards of God's Word comes at conversion.

CONTINUING PROGRESSIVE HOLINESS

Even though we are set apart to God, we fail often. We struggle to overcome the habits of sinful behavior. The truth that we are already seen as holy gives us encouragement as we seek to become holy. The second dimension of holiness is *progressive holiness*.

More Scriptures apply to everyday living than to our position before God. Most of the Epistles contain passages about how to implement the theology of conversion. God knows we have personal problems, sins, social prejudices, and religious questions. These require us to grow into what God expects. Actually, Christians hope to become better for good reasons.

WE ARE MADE IN GOD'S IMAGE

Because we as Christians are created in the image of God, we are born with the desire to become better people. Every person has inescapable moral direction within even though it is darkened by sin. Every person has a sense of right and wrong just by virtue of being human. The knowledge that we all share the same desire should be an encouragement in our individual pursuits of holiness. When people of any society reason together to formulate standards of behavior, they act on an inner sense of rightness that guides them. Paul called this the Law of God "written on [our] hearts" (Rom. 2:14-15). The human "laws" we construct simply reveal God's higher standards. At conversion, God's Holy Spirit builds on the natural moral instinct, giving it a more significant place in our lives. The Holy Spirit urges the believer toward being what God originally intended.

WE ARE SAVED FOR HOLINESS

Even the basic elements of conversion encourage us toward holiness. Several things incline persons to accept Christ. We must have a sense of sinfulness. Consciousness of sin brings realization of our separation from God. In addition, a proper understanding of sin brings knowledge that sin keeps us from realizing our full potential. Sin encourages us to act in ways we would rather not, and it produces patterns of living that harm others and ourselves. This twofold understanding—that sin offends God and that sin damages us—produces in us a deep desire to escape sin. Who would not want to change a life that brings God's judgment and at the same time causes great pain?

Who would not want to change a life that brings God's judgment and at the same time causes great pain?

This understanding then leads to repentance. The Greek word for *repentance* is *metanoia,* meaning "to change one's attitude." Many times we hear that repentance means to change one's mind, but the Greek word *noia* implies a much deeper concept. It connotes attitudes and dispositions. Repentance drives people to the attitude that they will do anything to change their lives in order to stop sinning.

33

The forgiveness offered by Jesus Christ brings the power we need to live as we ought.

The more deeply we analyze our life patterns and values, the more we realize we cannot change our attitudes to honor God. We need help. The desire to change prompts the cry for a Savior. That makes the gospel good news! God says we do not need to change our attitudes by ourselves, nor can we change the patterns of our lives by ourselves. Further, there is nothing we can do by ourselves to escape God's wrath which will be directed toward sin. No matter how much right we do, we cannot erase the wrong already done. It forever stands between God and us until we accept Jesus Christ. We need forgiveness of the past since we can do nothing to change it. The forgiveness offered by Jesus Christ brings the power we need to live as we ought.

Building on the conversion experience, the Bible consistently encourages Christians to be holy. Many New Testament passages teach Christians about practical holiness. The Epistles generally fall into a pattern. The first chapters discuss certain theological issues while the last chapters are devoted to applying those same theologies to one's life. In the broadest sense, all of the practical passages of the Epistles encourage us in holiness, since they call us to conform to God's values.

In many passages Paul urged Christians to live holy lives. For example, he used active commands to reinforce the necessity of obedience in Romans 6:12-13: "Therefore *do not let* sin reign in your mortal body so that you obey its evil desires. *Do not offer* the parts of your body to sin, as instruments of wickedness, but rather *offer* yourselves to God, as those who have been brought from death to life; and *offer* the parts of your body to him as instruments of righteousness" (italics added). In Galatians 5:19-21, He explained the importance of leaving the old life for the new:

> *The acts of the sinful nature are obvious: sexual immorality, impurity and debauchery; idolatry and witchcraft; hatred, discord, jealousy, fits of rage, self-*

ish ambition, dissensions, factions and envy; drunkenness, orgies, and the like. I warn you, as I did before, that those who live like this will not inherit the kingdom of God.

One of the most pointed commands in Paul's writings contrasts the way of the world with following Christ. In Romans 12:1-2, he said,

Therefore, I urge you, brothers, in view of God's mercy, to offer your bodies as living sacrifices, holy and pleasing to God–this is your spiritual act of worship. Do not conform any longer to the pattern of this world, but be transformed by the renewing of your mind. Then you will be able to test and approve what God's will is–his good, pleasing and perfect will.

Other writers provide similar encouragements. The apostle Peter wrote: "Therefore, prepare your minds for action; be self-controlled; set your hope fully on the grace to be given you when Jesus Christ is revealed. As obedient children, do not conform to the evil desires you had when you lived in ignorance" (1 Pet. 1:13-14). James, the half brother of our Lord, warned:

Submit yourselves, then, to God. Resist the devil, and he will flee from you. Come near to God and he will come near to you. Wash your hands, you sinners, and purify your hearts, you double-minded. Grieve, mourn and wail. Change your laughter to mourning and your joy to gloom. Humble yourselves before the Lord, and he will lift you up (Jas. 4:7-10).

John expressed this point as well. He said,

Do not love the world or anything in the world. If anyone loves the world, the love of the Father is not in him. For everything in the world–the cravings of

sinful man, the lust of his eyes and the boasting of what he has and does–comes not from the Father but from the world. The world and its desires pass away, but the man who does the will of God lives forever (1 John 2:15-17).

As a final example, the writer of Hebrews exhorts to holiness as well. In Hebrews 3:1, he acknowledged that his readers were positionally "holy." He said, "Therefore, holy brothers, who share in the heavenly calling, fix your thoughts on Jesus, the apostle and high priest whom we confess." At the same time he urged his readers on to practical holiness: "See to it, brothers, that none of you has a sinful, unbelieving heart that turns away from the living God. But encourage one another daily, as long as it is called Today, so that none of you may be hardened by sin's deceitfulness" (vv. 12-13).

His encouragements included a desire to be perfect, as he said, "Make every effort to live in peace with all men and to be holy; without holiness no one will see the Lord" (v. 14).

God's commands to be holy permeate the entire New Testament and clarify God's plan for the Christian.

These passages illustrate the fact that God's commands to be holy permeate the entire New Testament. Passages like these clarify God's plan for the Christian. Conversion is the beginning of a life devoted to overcoming sin, developing new values, and growing in holiness. There is a positional holiness in which God views Christians as already holy, and there is also a progressive holiness in which the Christian actually becomes what God intends.

ULTIMATE COMPLETE HOLINESS

God intends for believers to attain complete perfection, actually living without sin. Positional and progressive sanctification begin this process. While both have significant meaning, both leave the Christian dissatisfied. Positional sanctification views us from God's perspective, based on God's decree of justification. Progressive sanctification describes our progress toward personal sanctification. But sin continues to be a problem in life. The believer's heart cries for complete freedom from sin. We long for a situation where sin does not tempt us and where we can see God without the limitations sin imposes. These longings will be rewarded. The Bible promises complete holiness.

The doctrine of complete sanctification brings comfort and hope. Even if on earth we cannot escape the influence of sin, someday that will change. Complete sanctification brings ultimate victory for the believer. Since sinfulness and finiteness limit our ability to know God as we should, complete holiness brings complete knowledge and fellowship.

Complete sanctification brings ultimate victory for the believer.

Several passages of Scripture teach this aspect of holiness. One of the clearest is 1 John 3:2. John said, "Dear friends, now we are children of God, and what we will be has not yet been made known. But we know that when he appears, we shall be like him, for we shall see him as he is." This text and others suggest important truths about complete sanctification.

Release from sin occurs at the believer's death. At that time the limitations of sin are removed, and the believer goes immediately to be with the Lord in a perfect place. At that time the believer becomes morally perfect. Perfect character replaces life infected with sin. Yet there is more.

The completion of holiness is future. Completeness happens when we see Jesus. No one on earth fully understands what complete sanctification will be like. Complete sanctification comes with complete knowledge of Jesus which only occurs at the second coming.

Most Christians will be with Christ at that time, but we will be without our bodies. Complete sanctification includes more than the soul and spirit. It extends to the body as well. In writing to the Thessalonians, Paul prayed: "May God himself, the God of peace, sanctify you through and through. May your whole spirit, soul and body be kept blameless at the coming of our Lord Jesus Christ" (1 Thess. 5:23). The body will be transformed when Jesus comes again; believers leave behind the body which is naturally maintained and embrace the spiritually maintained body (see 1 Cor. 15:35-53). In the transformation process from natural to spiritual, the body is sanctified. Then God's plan for holiness reaches completion.

The body remains in the grave until the resurrection of the body which occurs when Jesus returns to earth. Before then, believers in heaven experience moral and spiritual holiness, but they await the joy of reunion with their glorified bodies. Jesus' power alone effects the change into His image. The verse, "We shall see him as he is" (1 John 3:2), suggests that we will be transformed by seeing Him.

The promise of victory encourages daily life. Romans 6:14 also teaches a future complete sanctification: "For sin shall not be your master, because you are not under law, but under grace." This verse concludes a discussion of the believer's death to sin and the command to present our bodies to God as instruments of righteousness. Obviously there is ultimate victory for the believer. The fact is, "sin shall not be your master." This is more than a statement of hope. It does not teach that if we make the correct choices we will gain victory over sin. It states clearly that sin will not rule over us.

We should live on earth consistent with our real character and destination: heaven and its perfection.

Since our final destiny is a life free from sin, Paul presented this truth as an incentive for making the correct choices on earth. It is both inconceivable and inconsistent for believers to choose to follow a life of sin here on earth when our salvation promises us a life of perfection someday. We should live on earth consistent with our real character and destination: heaven and its perfection.

PERSONAL LEARNING ACTIVITY

Do you struggle with consistency in your walk with Christ? What are the obstacles to consistent holy living in your life?

_____

_____

Pray that God will help you face and overcome these obstacles.

Romans 6:14 also provides the reason for the promise of holiness: "you are not under law, but under grace." Law brings its demands, accusations, and judgments. Since no one other than Jesus has ever lived correctly under law, every person can expect to be judged as a sinner. For Paul, judgment under law and the power of sin go hand in hand: "The sting of death is sin, and the power of sin is the law" (1 Cor. 15:56). Christians have been delivered from the power of sin in their lives, and they have died to law: "So, my brothers, you also died to the law through the body of Christ, that you might belong to another, to him who was raised from the dead, in order that we might bear fruit to God" (Rom. 7:4). Grace has done what the law could not do. Grace not only erases the sin of the past, but also it provides for the life of the future. Grace guarantees that sin will be defeated completely in the believer's life. Paul said: "The law was added so that the trespass might increase. But where sin increased, grace increased all the more, so that, just as sin reigned in death, so also grace might reign through righteousness to bring eternal life through Jesus Christ our Lord" (Rom. 5:20-21). Christians, now under grace, will receive the full blessings of salvation including complete victory over sin.

Grace guarantees that sin will be defeated completely in the believer's life.

God completes redemption when a believer experiences everything God intends.

These representative texts describe the ultimate goal of being like Christ. God completes redemption when a believer experiences everything God intends. We have already seen that God intends to bring believers into the fullness of the image of God. The New Testament clarifies what that means: it is being like Jesus.

In summary, holiness occurs in three stages. The believer is *positionally* holy at conversion. While living on earth the believer becomes *progressively* more holy through fellowship with Christ. Finally, believers anticipate *complete sanctification* when the Lord returns and resurrects the bodies of believers.

CONTEMPORARY EVANGELICAL APPROACHES TO SANCTIFICATION

Evangelical Christians have various theologies explaining how we achieve holiness in personal living. I will briefly survey four basic evangelical approaches to holiness. They correspond to four different theological and ecclesiastical positions that have developed through the centuries.

Each of the positions surveyed is evangelical. The categories are quite broad. The particular descriptions of these approaches to holiness do not mean that everyone who teaches that approach will agree on the finer points. I am attempting to simplify for the purpose of understanding.[2]

WESLEYAN APPROACH

Wesleyan theology comes from the great preacher and theologian John Wesley. The Wesleyan tradition encompasses many church groups, such as the Free Methodists, the Nazarenes, the Christian and Missionary Alliance, and the Salvation Army.

This approach also been known for its focus on social issues that are viewed as an integral part of Christian faith. This lies at the heart of the Wesleyan interpretation of Christianity, since, according to this theology, all mature believers demonstrate their relationship to Christ by the way they live.

Wesley believed that Christians can attain "complete perfection" on earth. This corresponds to Wesley's understanding that Christians should develop personal holiness. Perhaps more significantly for this study, they not only *should* develop it, but also they *can* develop it. The ability to attain "complete perfection" was the logical outworking of grace, regeneration, and faith motivated by love.

Wesleyans believe that the promise of sanctification occurs in both the Old and New Testaments. Wesley understood that the promise involved deliverance from all willful sin. These Old Testament passages are thought to teach this:

The Lord your God will circumcise your hearts and the hearts of your descendants, so that you may love him with all your heart and with all your soul, and live (Deut. 30:6).

I will sprinkle clean water on you, and you will be clean; I will cleanse you from all your impurities and from all your idols (Ezek. 36:25).

The corollaries in the New Testament are passages such as:

For what the law was powerless to do in that it was weakened by the sinful nature, God did by sending his own Son in the likeness of sinful man to be a sin offering. And so he condemned sin in sinful man, in order that the righteous requirements of the law might be fully met in us, who do not live according to the sinful nature but according to the Spirit (Rom. 8:3-4).

In this way, love is made complete among us so that

we will have confidence on the day of judgment, because in this world we are like him (1 John 4:17).

The Wesleyans consider deliverance from sin as deliverance from any *known* sin. That is, the Christian could reach a state of sinlessness regarding any known violation of a law. Sinless perfection does not include Christians feeling the influence of ignorance, mistakes, infirmities, and involuntary temptations.[3] In order to reach sinless perfection, Christians must have a crisis experience. Unlike the beliefs of Pentecostals, this second experience includes a definite act of faith.

This tradition focuses on two experiential points of a Christian's life: justification and sanctification. The two experiences have different motivations and outworkings. Justification brings regeneration and conversion. Sanctification brings complete victory over sin.

PENTECOSTAL APPROACH

Pentecostalism developed into two distinct movements. The earlier grew out of a Wesleyan tradition and has many similarities to the Wesleyan approach to sanctification. The second came from various traditions that do not reflect the distinctives of the Wesleyans.

Can Christians live sinlessly?

The differences in the two wings of the movement basically involve one point: Can Christians live sinlessly? Those whose history includes the Wesleyan tradition argue that Christians can achieve a state of freedom from known sin. The others believe that such a state is impossible.

All Pentecostals believe in a baptism of the Holy Spirit that brings the ability to witness effectively. The pro-Wesleyan group believes that the filling of the Holy Spirit comes to those who are already mature. They are sinless. Thus, it is a third stage of spiritual development following conversion and sanctification. The other group believes in the baptism of the Holy Spirit following conversion that brings power for purity and effective proclamation of the gospel.

The initial evidence of the filling of the Spirit is the ability to speak in tongues, although that is only one evidence. Many of them point to Acts 2:4 which describes how the Holy Spirit came on the early church. They see this as normative for all believers. Pentecostals say Christians today should seek the baptism of the Holy Spirit, and they will recognize the Spirit's presence by comparing the phenomena in their lives to the experience of the church in Acts 2.

All Pentecostals agree that the baptism of the Spirit brings a new ability to become holy. No one can be what God desires without that experience.

All of them were filled with the Holy Spirit and began to speak in other tongues as the Spirit enabled them.
Acts 2:4

KESWICK APPROACH

The Keswick teaching of holiness gets its name from a series of meetings that began in 1875 in Keswick, England. In America, the term *Keswick* identifies a message often called the victorious life. Keswick cannot be confined to any denomination. The Keswick teachers were powerful, articulate persons who gained a significant following both because of their oratory and the power of their message.

Keswick theology basically teaches two stages of growth. The first is conversion. Many Christians know nothing more than conversion. They often live their lives like their non-Christian neighbors because they simply do not know anything different. Because of that, the "average" Christian is constantly overcome by temptation and sin. Average Christians are likely to live like the church at Corinth which was carnal or like Paul's self-description in Romans 7:14-25. Both texts express the fact that Christians can be carnal; they can live just like the world from which they came.

The answer to this is a second spiritual experience. This experience involves recognizing that the Christian is dead to sin. Because of death to sin, every Christian should make a conscious act of commitment of the whole person to Christ, with a prayer of faith that God will provide victory. This theology stresses a "normal" Christian life. The normal life is far from the average Christian life. The average Christian struggles, hoping to live up to the expectations that come at conversion. Through a second experience, subsequent to conversion, Christians can move from average to normal. The normal Christian life brings great blessings.

The believer must get out of the way and allow Jesus to live through him.

Keswick teachers presented the idea of "life and death" as the basis of victory. For most Keswick preachers, the way to life is death. The way to unleash the power that brings victory is to "die." Every believer must die to sin. This is normally interpreted as a second experience after salvation. After the believer dies to sin, the emphasis on death means that he should die anew. This means that we reaffirm our condition of being dead to sin. Basically the believer must get out of the way and allow Jesus to live through him. Progress in the Christian life comes by yielding oneself to Jesus, expressed as death to sin, and allowing Christ to live through our lives day by day. One distinguishing phrase of Keswick theologians is "death to self; alive to God." Death to sin means that believers must count on the fact that they have died to sin. Further, they must live a life of obedience, normally referred to as the "crucified life." The power of Christ is unleashed when the believer dies to sin, allowing Jesus to live through him or her. The two unique key terms of Keswick theology are *death* and *Christ within*.

REFORMED APPROACH

The Reformed tradition derives its name from John Calvin (d. 1564) and his followers. The Reformed tradition has gained strength in the centuries since Calvin lived. However, while there are basic similarities among the Reformers, there was not a clear teaching on sanctification. It is difficult to identify one strain of teaching that all Reformed theologians will accept. It will be best, therefore, to identify what characterizes the Reformed position.

Reformed theology distinguishes between justification and sanctification. Justification is a one-time act that frees a sinner from the guilt of sin at the time of conversion. Sanctification is a process whereby God removes the pollution of sin. The process involves continual cooperation with the Holy Spirit in a progressive sanctification. The Reformed approach to sanctification does not include a second experience. Rather, the Christian life is a day-by-day struggle with sin. The believer should expect victory over sin, but it will not come in a way that immediately brings success. Nearly always the classic Reformed writers confess days of prayer and agonizing with God to find the peace of victory. The more believers know Christ, the more they have an awareness of sin. Struggling with sin is quite compatible with progress toward purity.

The Reformed tradition affirms the role of the Holy Spirit in the believer's life. Reformed theologians consistently point out that the Holy Spirit brings the power to overcome sin. The basic Christian responsibility is to cooperate with the work of the Holy Spirit enabling progress.

Reformed theologians disagree on the definition of the new nature. The question is whether the old nature continues in the life of the believer. Augustine and Calvin held to the position that the believer has two natures within. More recent theologians in this tradition hold to the position that the believer has only one nature. The "two-nature approach" takes the position that the Holy Spirit progressively enables the new nature to dominate the old. The "one-nature approach" takes the position that the believer's life is progressively transformed into a lifestyle consistent with the new nature given at conversion.

The question is whether the old nature continues in the life of the believer.

The Reformed tradition believes that a Christian will continue to sin until death. Christians will not be able to overcome sin completely and display a life of purity on the earth. They always will have a struggle with sin until they reach the deliverance that comes when they see Christ. In the meantime, the Holy Spirit brings power to overcome and experience holiness.

CONCLUSION

Only holiness pleases God and represents Christ to the world.

Christians differ on the specifics of how to become holy. Yet we find unity in one major concern. All agree that Christians should live holy lives displaying the purity of Christian character. Only holiness pleases God and truly represents Christ to the world around us.

PERSONAL LEARNING ACTIVITY

The author states that "Christians should live holy lives displaying the purity of Christian character." At this moment, stop and pray that this study will stir believers everywhere to seek to be holy in the power of God's Spirit.

---

[1]David Peterson makes a valid distinction between sanctification and holiness. In general he uses the terms as follows: *sanctification* is what God does for us at conversion; *holiness* is our responsibility to live the implications of sanctification. While his point is helpful, it seems that the Bible uses sanctification in present terms as an incentive to overcome sin (see 1 Thess. 4:3-6). Further, the distinction is largely based on the English translations of the Greek words for *sanctification* and *holiness*. Maintaining the distinction completely seems unsupportable in some contexts where the textual environment supports the present use. Nevertheless, David Peterson's book is of great value, and I am in basic agreement with it. See David Peterson, *Possessed by God. A New Testament Theology of Sanctification and Holiness* (Grand Rapids, Mich.: William B. Eerdmans Publishing Co., 1995), 12-14.

[2]There are many helpful references for understanding the positions that will be briefly described in what follows. Some of the most helpful because of brevity, accuracy, and interaction among advocates of various positions are: Melvin E. Dieter, Anthony A. Hoekema, Stanley M. Horton, J. Robertson McQuilkin, and John F. Walvoord, *Five Views on Sanctification* (Grand Rapids, Mich.: Zondervan Publishing House, 1987); Bruce Demarest, "Transformed into His Likeness," in *The Cross and Salvation* (Wheaton, Ill.: Crossway Books, 1997), 385-429; D. L. Alexander, ed., *Christian Spirituality: Five Views of Sanctification* (Downer's Grove, Ill.: InterVarsity Press, 1988); and the standard theology textbooks.

[3]Demarest, *The Cross and Salvation*, 391.

Personal Transformation

WHO AM I?

Christians ought to be different. Whether we like it or not we have a responsibility when we profess Christ. People expect that Christians will never lose their temper, never become impatient, never curse, gossip, complain, or do anything else wrong. The common expectation is that upon conversion to Christ there will be a new way of living.

As Christians we react to this expectation. We realize that we have a strong tendency to sin. We know the struggles we have within. Further, we know that temptations to sin grow stronger once we identify with Christ. At times we wish unbelievers understood those dynamics and had more sympathy for our problems. The fact is they don't.

An even more important issue than how others perceive us is what the Bible teaches. If we desire comfort in living sinful lives, we will not find it in the Bible. The standards in God's Word are high. God expects His people to be holy, set apart to Him and from the world. He expects that the patterns of the pre-Christian life will be replaced with new lifestyles.

On the other hand, God understands failure. For that reason there are many passages of Scripture explaining how we are to grow in Christ and what to do when we fail. One thing is certain: God loves us, and His love will never change. He loves us equally when we fail and when we succeed.

We find a constant tension in our lives. On the one hand we desire to be like Christ. We understand the sinful dispo-

One thing is certain—God loves us, and His love will never change.

47

sition that characterized us before conversion, and we wish to be as holy and pure as possible. On the other hand, there are constant battles with sin. So what is new about a believer? Since God begins His work in our minds, we cannot grow without understanding who we are. But this understanding alone will not bring victory over sin or the holiness that we desire.

Earlier I mentioned the concern some express about terminology. Does sanctification refer only to the work of the Holy Spirit at conversion and the culmination of purification at the second coming? Those who make this distinction prefer to use the word *holiness* strictly in regard to the life we live. For the most part this distinction is based on which is the better English word for a given context: *sanctification* or *holiness*. I take the position that transformation is very much a part of holiness. It is also the product of sanctification.

Being set apart for God means that we will live according to God's plan based on His holy character.

We need an understanding of what holiness looks like while avoiding a specific "list approach" to godly living, because the lists will change from place to place and time to time. On the other hand, basic principles transcend time and place. God puts this framework in place at conversion. The principles are intuitional for new believers but not all Christians grasp them. Believers may fail at many points and not achieve the happiness of holy living. Being set apart for God means that we will live according to God's plan based on His holy character. Sometimes it is best to explain it as living by God's economy rather than our own. The more we are able to live out our conversion experience in life, the more we will be fulfilled and at peace.

Therefore, the principles of Christian life presented in this section are not "add ons" to conversion. They are not optional. They come at conversion with regeneration, and God expects us to grow consistently from that point forward. A change of life involves a change of self-identity, and that means we must understand who we really are.

**Close your eyes. Recall a time when you
struggled with a temptation to sin. Now
recall an experience when you spoke up
for Christ and His kingdom. Consider how
these thoughts and feelings differ.
In the margin list ways you have grown
from these experiences.**

OLD PERSON/NEW PERSON

The Bible uses several terms to describe the Christian's experience as new. Perhaps the most clearly stated is 2 Corinthians 5:17: "Therefore, if anyone is in Christ, he is a new creation; the old has gone, the new has come!" Most people understand this verse to mean that when a person accepts Christ, a new life begins. More recently, many scholars interpret it to express Paul's hope that a new age has come. Taking this view, Paul stated that at his conversion he entered the new age ushered in by Jesus' death and resurrection. Both seem to stress the fact that something new happens to a believer. What is that newness?

FROM THE OLD TO THE NEW

Paul described in three places the change which occurs in a believer as he or she moves from the old person to the new person (see Rom. 6:6; Eph. 4:22; and Col. 3:9-10). Paul expressed the change as from the old man to the new man. The Greek word for *man, anthropos,* is a general word often meaning "humanity." It includes both man and woman. How does this word express a biblical understanding of personal transformation? The use of the word *man* prompts the issue of the old nature and the new nature. What is the old man compared with the new man? Some modern translations translate this as "self."

49

NEW TESTAMENT DESCRIPTIONS

Do not lie to each other, since you have taken off your old self with its practices and have put on the new self, which is being renewed in knowledge in the image of its Creator.
Colossians 3:9-10

The most instructive passage is Colossians 3:9-10. It parallels Ephesians 4:22 and compliments Romans 6:6. In this section of Colossians, Paul explained how to live consistently with conversion. He described who Jesus is (see 1:9-23) and what Jesus' death means to those who follow Christ (see 2:6–3:4). Paul then turned to the practical implications of the Christian life—including practical holiness.

Christians are to "put to death, therefore, whatever belongs to your earthly nature" (3:5). These things are explained in two groups of five—one personal and one social. The personal concerns are: "sexual immorality, impurity, lust, evil desires and greed, which is idolatry" (v. 5). The social concerns are: "anger, rage, malice, slander, and filthy language" (v. 8). A final concern regards lying. Christians are not to "lie to each other" (v. 9). Lying has no place in God's economy.

Paul gave a reason for turning away from the characteristics of the old life: "Since you have taken off your old self with its practices and have put on the new self" (3:9-10). The verse indicates a decisive change The command to "put to death" (v. 5) was impossible without this change. Two important points emerge. First, Paul based his commands to holy living on their conversion experience. He did not tell them "to die to self." That occurred when they chose to identify with Christ and His death (see Rom. 6:1-4). It is further instructive that Paul never used the term *die to self* as any explanation of how to live the Christian life. When he used the metaphor of death, it was to end the activities that characterize the former life. Second, it appears that the church at Colosse was not yet completely holy. If not, his commands would have no relevance. But they had been changed whether or not the new self appeared as the dominant characteristic of their lives. Converted people may still be quite sinful in their actions, yet they have experienced salvation. Both of these points help us to understand that death to self was a past experience for these believers.

On the other hand, this passage reveals that the past experience leads to an ongoing change in life. The need to grow is further emphasized by verse 10 where Paul explained that the new self "is being renewed in knowledge in the image of its Creator." Even the new self cannot claim perfection. Rather, it must constantly be transformed to become holy. The goal, being like the Creator, is the end of a process beginning with knowledge. The Colossians were in process.

The goal, being like the Creator, is the end of a process beginning with knowledge.

We can glean the logical sequence of events in conversion from this passage. These events are: 1) taking off the old self; 2) putting on the new self; and 3) being renewed in knowledge of the Creator. From the language used here, it appears that the old self and new self are incompatible. That is, they do not coexist. Otherwise, *putting off* and *putting on* make no sense. Further, the transactions of putting off and putting on do not preclude the necessity of growth. Thus, there is a twofold dynamic. One is conversion, at which time the old person is put off. The other is the ongoing transformation of life that takes place through knowledge.

In the parallel passage, Ephesians chapter 4, Paul contrasted the life of the Gentiles with the life of Christians. Paul identified the Gentiles here because they represented the way godless people live. After explaining a lifestyle of immorality and insensitivity to God, Paul complimented the church for the change of behavior that occurred at conversion. In 4:20 he stated, "You, however, did not come to know Christ that way." He took them back mentally to their conversion experience. At the time of their conversion they knew better than to continue living as the Gentiles lived. Paul made this explicit in 4:22-24: "You were taught, with regard to your former way of life, to put off your old self, which is being corrupted by its deceitful desires; to be made new in the attitude of your minds; and to put on the new self, created to be like God in true righteousness and holiness."

The primary difference between this passage and the one in Colossians is the sequence of events. In Ephesians Paul stressed the truth that growth in knowledge was a part of salvation. More precisely, he used the word *attitude* rather than *knowledge* (the Greek word is *noos*). At conversion the Ephesians had a change of attitude regarding the "old person" and the "new person." This change of attitude led them to embrace the values of the "new person." Something new happened at conversion. Although some will read the words *to put off* as future and therefore relevant to a Christian's postconversion life, in actuality the context reveals that Paul used the words to make it past. The entire context speaks of knowledge that enabled them to come to a point of salvation. Further, like Colossians, there is an antithesis between the old self and the new self. They do not coexist.

In the same way, count yourselves dead to sin but alive to God in Christ Jesus.
Romans 6:11

The third passage employing the "old person" terminology is Romans 6. In verse 6 Paul stated, "For we know that our old self was crucified with him." Once again the verbs are past tense. Paul described something that happened at their conversion. The point of Romans 6:1-14 is to help the "new self" live consistently in light of the conversion experience. Again, the passage reveals that the "old self" and the "new self" do not coexist.

The three passages have a consistency of expression in the use of "old person/new person" terminology. The change from the old man to a new man takes place at conversion, and the two "selves" do not coexist.

PERSONAL LEARNING ACTIVITY

How is a Christian's life different from the lives of people who have yet to invite Christ into their hearts?

_____

ONE NATURE OR TWO?

There are a significant number of people who teach that both old self and new self are present in believers. Their arguments arise basically from two sources: Scripture and Christian experience. Regarding the first, there are multiple passages that explain the continuing spiritual battle in the lives of Christians. Paul said, for example, that we must put to death our members and activities that are the vehicles for sin (see Eph. 4:25; Col. 3:5). Even though we have put off the old person and put on the new, we must continually reinforce that action by "putting off" the activities of the old person and "putting on" the new activities. The command to put to death the deeds of the flesh implies the need to complete something already accomplished.

Therefore each of you must put off falsehood and speak truthfully to his neighbor, for we are all members of one body.
Ephesians 4:25

Those who argue for the presence of two natures within a believer also point out important experiential characteristics. All believers struggle with an inward pull toward sin. How are we to explain the tendency to sin if the "old person" is no longer resident within? The experiential argument provides a powerful explanation for believers continuing to sin. After all, the tendency to sin originated in the "old person."

Neither of these arguments explains Scripture well. As for the biblical basis for the "two-nature" explanation, the language of the Bible clearly distinguishes between the change at conversion and the changes expected because of conversion. The "death" terminology generally applies to learning to live after conversion. Christians "put to death" certain sinful activities and attitudes. In other words, our lives should conform to what has actually happened to us. This language fits perfectly with the tension already seen between sanctification as positional and sanctification as progressive.

The experiential argument for the "two-nature" theory calls for careful thought as well. It is true that even Christian people sin. Since such sinful acts and attitudes are identified

Who are the "old person" and the "new person" anyway?

with the "old person," it stands to reason that some think the "old person" still lives in the believer. However, such reasoning does not fit the language of Scripture. In fact, Scripture teaches that the reason to "put to death" sinfully motivated acts is because they are inconsistent with who we really are. We really are the "new person." "New people" should not act like "old people." This leads to an important question: Who are the "old person" and the "new person" anyway? In Pauline thought the "old person" question has been answered from several perspectives which follow.

First, it has been approached theologically. Those who take a theological approach often equate the "old person" to a *positional* truth that the old life is past. Second, "old person" has also been interpreted psychologically. Viewed from this perspective, the "old person" is a *nature*. The Bible does use the word *nature* to explain why unbelievers act as they do (see Eph. 2:3), but such use is rare. There is little to suggest that the "old person" and "nature" are to be equated. Third, the term has been approached from a philosophical perspective. There are some who equate the term *old person* to the *substance* of human beings. Those who approach it this way often argue that something real, "the substance" or something about our actual beings changes at conversion. Fourth, the phrase has also been interpreted historically. In this approach, the "old person" refers to a period of time, or, better, a situation in the believer's life. Those who understand the phrase this way point out the historical sequences of movement from one situation called unbelief to another called faith. Finally, some theologians understand this eschatologically. They teach that the terms are corporate or economical. The "old person" is the present evil age while the "new person" is the age of salvation ushered in by Jesus Christ. This final position interprets all of the texts above corporately rather than individually, and that individuals find themselves in the new age because of Christ. As part of the "new person," believers should live pure lives.

Most of the discussion regarding sanctification revolves around two possible interpretations. The questions are: Are there two "natures" within a believer? If so, what are they? If not, how do we explain Paul's terminology?

TWO-NATURE APPROACH

Those who hold to the position that a believer has two natures generally find support in the early church fathers. Augustine (d. 430) is usually credited with developing the idea. There are some variations (as is the case with any position described generically). Nevertheless, the basic idea is as follows. The two natures within believers correspond to the two experiences of Christians. The believer used to be in an unregenerate state. That is described as "in Adam," "in the flesh," or the "old man." The first nature, therefore, comes from Adam and is passed through birth to every person. That nature is characterized by self-orientation and a strong love of sin. It is decidedly anti-God and contrary to His purposes. It characterizes every non-Christian. At conversion the believer in Christ receives a new nature. This new nature corresponds to the new life at conversion, and the new nature comes from Christ. This new nature is characterized by a God-orientation and a desire to be submissive to Christ. It loves holiness and purity.

Only Christians possess the new nature. Yet Christians also possess the old nature. This means that in every believer there remains a love of and tendency toward sin. The old nature explains the constant struggle with sin and the sensitivity to temptation. At the same time, there is within a hatred for sin and a love of God because of the new nature. Having both of these natures means that there is a constant battle between them. Because of the intensity of the battle, we need an arbitrator who determines what the person actually does. The arbitrator is the Holy Spirit. The Spirit fights against the old nature so that the new nature can dominate. Believers who allow the Holy Spirit to control their lives display the work of the Spirit.

The Holy Spirit fights against the old nature so that the new nature can dominate.

55

ONE-NATURE APPROACH

Those who teach that a person has only one nature differ at several main points with the two-nature approach. Like the two-nature proponents, they contend that unbelievers have only one nature. It is a disposition that embraces sin and actions that are contrary to God. It is the residue of Adam's sin passed down to all persons. At conversion the old nature is changed so that it embraces God. Still learning new life patterns takes time, so change comes progressively throughout the believer's new life. Even so, God implants a deep desire to be obedient and to follow a life of holiness.

The question is: Why do we sin?

The central issue in this approach is: Why do we sin? Those who hold to one nature explain that the believer's nature progressively changes. Conversion does not mean that the believer cannot sin. It only means that the believer no longer wants to sin. The Holy Spirit brings the power to change one's nature. As the believer cooperates with the work of the Spirit, the believer's nature is changed into the purity of what God expects. Therefore the one nature—the only nature we will ever have—is transformed toward holiness.

PROBLEMS WITH THE TWO-NATURE APPROACH

Many good and powerful Christians hold to some form of the two-nature position. Nevertheless, it seems that Scripture teaches a unified nature of all persons, including believers. Accepting a two-nature approach to the essence of Christians raises basic problems that are biblical, soteriological (relating to the theology of salvation), psychological, and eschatological (relating to the theology of end times).

BIBLICAL ISSUES

The Bible never uses the word *nature* in describing two different motivations toward life. In Ephesians 2:3 Paul did speak of the Gentiles who do "by nature" sinful acts. He also attributed immorality and idolatry to a "natural" state of unbelievers. On the other hand, the Bible never talks about a "new nature" being given to anyone. The only use of the term *nature* in relation to believers occurs in 2 Peter 1:4. There Peter described believers as those who "participate in the divine nature and escape the corruption in the world caused by evil desires." This text probably has a future reference consistent with its context. It teaches that God has given us great promises that will empower us to escape the corruption of the world–someday–and share in the divine nature. Verses 5 through 9 exhort the believer to develop Christian virtues as the most certain protection from being entrapped in the corruption of the world. Thus, Scripture's clear testimony speaks of only one nature when the word *nature* is used.

Through these he has given us his very great and precious promises, so that through them you may participate in the divine nature and escape the corruption in the world caused by evil desires. 2 Peter 1:4

SOTERIOLOGICAL ISSUES

The two-nature theory also raises questions about the nature of regeneration. Orthodox Christians have always affirmed the fact that at conversion regeneration takes place in the unbeliever. Substantial discussion relates to the issue of *what* is regenerated. For our purposes here the question must be asked of the human nature. Is it regenerated? Rather than affirming a substantive change in a person at conversion, the two-nature approach simply states that at conversion God gives a new nature. The position basically affirms that God adds to the person rather than transforms what already exists. That raises serious questions as to what is changed in the old person.

PSYCHOLOGICAL ISSUES

Accepting the two-nature theory also raises questions about Christian victory. If the two natures war against each other at every decisive point of temptation, then who determines which nature wins and how does that nature win? The two-nature theory leaves the "person" as a neutral observer of two powers or at least the influences within. The believer is passive and neutral, a non-participant in the battle but very much affected by the strength of both natures. Christians are never encouraged to be passive about the Christian life. Some suggest that one nature defeats the other because of the choices we make. That is, if a Christian chooses the old nature's actions, it wins, and vice versa. But what or who influences the choice? The response may well be that the Holy Spirit does. Even so, with this approach the person does not overcome, the nature does.

ESCHATOLOGICAL ISSUES

The two-nature approach raises questions as to *what* is finally redeemed and transformed when the believer is called to heaven. Is part of the believer left behind—the old nature that never submitted to Christ? Which part of the person is that? Unless the old nature is redeemed, then victory over sin does not include the original person—the sin nature—who was the problem. Scripture teaches that believers will be transformed, and the entire person—everything he or she is—will be carried to heaven. This begins at conversion, continues at the death of a believer, and is completed at the resurrection. Is only the "new nature" a part of the resurrection? Since the two-nature position separates the natures from the person, these questions are inevitable. Every believer has thoughts and actions that are more characteristic of the old person than the new.

> **Scripture teaches that believers will be transformed, and the entire person—everything he or she is—will be carried to heaven.**

PERSONAL LEARNING ACTIVITY

This section teaches that "believers will be transformed, and the entire person—everything he or she is—will be carried to heaven." Are there facets of your life that are not fit for heaven? How is this study on holiness helping you to deal with these issues in your life?

_____

_____

VALIDATIONS OF THE ONE-NATURE APPROACH

The one-nature approach corresponds better to the biblical teaching about sanctification and to Christian experience. Perhaps this can be seen clearly in light of the issues identified as problems with the two-nature approach.

BIBLICAL ISSUES

What does the Bible teach? All facets of the subject cannot be explored fully; neither can the biblical data be presented in its entirety. Nevertheless, this is basic to the doctrine of holiness, and therefore an overview will be helpful. We will review the three primary stages of human development: preconversion, postconversion, and the eternal state.

The three primary stages of human development are: preconversion, postconversion, and the eternal state.

PRECONVERSION

The preconversion situation is clear. Many New Testament passages speak of the unbeliever as limited by the "Adam only" existence (see Rom. 5:12-21). In Adam the entire person has a disposition to sin. Indeed, everything done by the unbeliever is touched by sin and is usually evidenced by a central egocentricity that understands the world as revolving around me and my interests. The blinding effects of sin, what theologians call the noetic effects, keep us from understanding what God really expects from us. Passages such as Romans 1:18–3:20 (esp. 3:9-20); 5:12-21; Ephesians 2:1-3, and 11-13 express this clearly. Often the writers of the Bible describe this as "in Adam," "the old man," and sometimes "the flesh." Without doubt, the preconversion person may be described as having a sinful nature.

POSTCONVERSION

The postconversion situation receives the most discussion in the Bible. At conversion there is an immediate change that leads to an ongoing progressive change of behavior: a person puts off the old person and puts on the new. The passages already discussed (see Rom. 6:6; Eph. 4:22-24; and

Col. 3:9-10) indicate that this happens. Ephesians uses the words, "put off" the old. Colossians states it as "taken off," while Romans uses the word "crucified." All speak to a separation from the past. The believer is no longer bound to the patterns of the past. The guilt of sin is removed, and there are new motivations, goals, and ambitions.

A progressive change of behavior comes as a believer acts in accord with salvation.

The progressive change of behavior comes as a believer acts in accord with salvation. The passages that speak of putting off the old person also speak of the need to conquer the sinful acts that characterized the past. Thus in Colossians, Paul used two metaphors to describe the believer's responsibility. In 3:5 he said, "put to death, therefore, whatever belongs to your earthly nature." This has been variously explained in history. Some have taken it almost literally, thinking that the best form of holiness was achieved by actual physical abuse of the body. But Paul did not decry physical comfort or health. Health and comfort are not the basic enemies of holiness. Others have understood this to mean that they were to put their personhood to death. These people decry personality, ambition, energy, and anything that brings the personal satisfaction of achievement. They say anything that allows "my person" to be prominent is contrary to God's will. Death, after all, means nonexistence.

A better understanding is that Paul wrote figuratively. The language is strong, but appropriate. The activities identified are not to predominate as they did before. Using forceful language, the Bible states that the believer is to do whatever possible to remove any trace of these in his life.

The second metaphor is translated by the *New International Version* as "whatever belongs to your earthly nature." The Greek literally is "members." Normally, the Greek word *mele* referred to bodily parts. It was extended to include activities that are promoted by the physical body. It is not unusual for Paul to explain the members as activities which he does in what follows. They are to put to death "sexual immorality, impurity, lust, evil desires and greed … anger, rage, malice, slander, and filthy language" (3:5,8). This suggests that the body promoted these activities in the past. The "old person" did these things because of who he was and how he used his "parts" (members).

At conversion, things change. The old person no longer exists. That means that the activities associated with his way of doing things should cease. We are to cease the old person's way of doing things by a conscious choice on our part and the divine help of the Holy Spirit.

The Ephesians passage speaks to the same issues even though the context reveals the issues are to be understood in relationship to the church. There is a corporate focus. Even so, the group cannot progress as it should without the individuals being what they should. Ephesians contrasts the preconversion experience (see 4:17-19) with postconversion expectations (see 4:20–6:20). Since they learned "to put off the old self" and to "put on the new" (see 4:22-24), they should devote themselves to stopping preconversion sinful activities and to promoting attitudes that encourage the new life.

In Romans 6:1-14, Paul addressed the problem of life-transformation. All Christians should apply the meaning of the cross to their own lives. Christians identify with Christ in death and resurrection (see 6:1-5). This means that at conversion we died "with Christ," enabling us to live a new life. The sequence of thought involves a purpose, an illustration, and some commands for the believer.

The purpose of our identification with Christ in death and resurrection is to overcome sin as taught in Romans 6:6. Three phrases occur sequentially, and each one depends on the phrase that preceded it. Paul started with "our old self was crucified with him." He continued with "that the body of sin might be done away with." There is less unanimity on the meaning of this phrase. Many understand it as synony-

The purpose of our identification with Christ in death and resurrection is to overcome sin.

61

*Put to death, therefore,
whatever belongs to your
earthly nature: sexual
immorality, impurity, lust, evil
desires and greed, which
is idolatry.
Colossians 3:5*

mous with the "old man" being crucified. But the Greek language will not comfortably allow that interpretation. It signifies the direct purpose of the crucifixion of the old man. Some have taken this to mean that the physical body should be eliminated. Stopping short of death, they have mutilated and buffeted their bodies into conformity. Others have understood the body of sin as the "mass" of sin, that is, sin in its entirety. It is best to understand this as the body "characterized by sin." This fits the injunctions of Colossians 3:5. Here Paul taught that the old person's crucifixion should lead to the ceasing of using our bodies for sin and its purposes.

The ultimate goal is that "we should no longer be slaves to sin." Slavery means complete obedience out of obligation. When sin is the master, as it is for all persons born into this world, it demands complete obedience. But the crucifixion of the old person should lead to a new freedom to act in accord with God's will so that sin's dominance is broken.

An illustration of the believer's death to sin draws on the analogy already presented. The believer has died, been buried, and raised with Christ (see Rom. 6:1-3). Such a death is a one-time experience (see 6:9) both for Christ and for the believer. After death, there is resurrection life that lasts forever without interruption brought by death. Jesus "died to sin" (6:10), and the believer died in the same way. The illustration draws a parallel that helps us understand the nature of the death to sin experience at conversion. Jesus died voluntarily to sin. He put Himself "under sin" to defeat sin in death. The unbeliever lives under sin. Unlike Christ, the unbeliever is dominated and influenced by it. But the believer's death is equated to Christ's death to sin. When He died, we died with Him. Our death to sin must be like His death to sin.

This is a "judicial" description. It's a reality that occurs spiritually now—to be completed at the time of the resurrection from the dead. Nevertheless, it brings power in this life so that it is the basis of all future transformation. At conversion, God breathes into our old man the breath of new life and enables the new man to thrive. These three passages describe immediate changes at conversion. The commands ensure progressive changes after our initial experience.

PERSONAL LEARNING ACTIVITY

Romans 6:6 says that our "old self was crucified with Him ... so that we would no longer be slaves to sin." Are you still a slave to sin? Has this great truth been a part of your quest for holiness? Explain why you believe that as a Christian you are no longer a slave to sin.

_____

_____

THE ETERNAL STATE

Having discussed the preconversion and postconversion states, consider the third—the eternal state. The entrance into the eternal state has two phases. The believer enters heaven to be with Christ immediately upon death. This is a full state of consciousness, and it includes all of the nonphysical aspects of the person. The second phase occurs at the resurrection. The resurrection of the dead occurs at the second coming of Christ. Until that time the body remains on earth or in the grave (see 1 Thess. 4:13-18; 1 Cor. 15:35-58). When Jesus comes, the struggle with sin will be over, and Christians will live in complete holiness with Christ forever.

We believe that Jesus died and rose again and so we believe that God will bring with Jesus those who have fallen asleep in him.
1 Thessalonians 4:14

SOTERIOLOGICAL ISSUES

In the two-nature approach a new nature is given to the believer, and this new nature coexists with the already present old nature. We questioned whether this was true to the doctrine of regeneration.

Regeneration comes from the words that mean "to be born again." A very important question relates to what actually is regenerated. The opening of eyes to spiritual sight is a change in the unbeliever. It is a work of the Holy Spirit in the old person enabling a response to the Spirit in repentance and faith, thereby becoming the new man. To say that regeneration simply brings the new nature is to imply that God somehow implants the new nature without regard to the old. This does not conform to Scripture. It seems best to understand that the old man is renewed and regenerated and that enables the new man to replace the old.

PSYCHOLOGICAL ISSUES

Earlier we raised the question as to whether the two-nature theory actually conforms to a biblical psychology. The problem is that it makes the person the "playing field" rather than a participant in the game itself. The one-nature approach locates change in the individual and, in part, as the responsibility of the individual. This does not suggest that the individual has power to effect the changes necessary for Christian growth, but it does mean that no growth will occur without a conscious choice of the believer.

The entire New Testament assumes that Christians are responsible for their growth in holiness. All of this together suggests that the old person becomes the new person as God begins His work of transformation at conversion.

ESCHATOLOGICAL ISSUES

Finally, there are concerns about the nature of the resurrected person. If there are two natures within a Christian, are they both transformed when we see Christ or is only one? The assumption is that the new nature is completed at that time, and the old nature is completely gone. One of the basic themes of redemption is that God redeems every facet of creation touched by sin. Redeeming only the new nature causes concerns. Does the new nature need redemption? The old nature is incapable of any progress toward holiness.

A basic theme of redemption is that God redeems every facet of creation touched by sin.

64

Only a portion of the total person would be redeemed if only the new nature feels the impact of redemption. Second, only a portion of the Christian person would enter heaven and enjoy the blessings of salvation. The old nature, a continuing part of the person, is left behind at that time. Both of these suggest that the new person must have direct relational ties to the old person.

THE FRUSTRATION FACTOR

So far, all of this has not addressed the core of the old man and the new man. It will be helpful to identify what actually changes. The old person has a characteristic way of doing things; he is blinded by sin and motivated by self-interests. Consequently, every action revolves around self and is sinful. The old person is the way a believer lived before salvation.

Basically, all of life before Christ is blinded by darkness and soiled by sin. This does not mean that a non-Christian is incapable of doing good things. The image of God in us motivates us to good actions both individually and socially. Paul explained this in Romans 2. He discussed the possibility that people who do not know God's will (the law) can actually do the things commanded in the law (see vv. 14-15). This includes individual choices (see vv. 1-3) as well as the standards any particular society establishes as its norms for conduct (see v. 15).

The image of God in us motivates us to good actions both individually and socially.

On the other hand, at conversion things change. New life is far more complex. We have times of victory, times of defeat, and times of ambivalence. Even so, in the core of our being, we desire to know God and to be like Him because of regeneration.

The new person is everything one is and can be as a Christian. This includes a new motivation, new ambitions, new attitudes, new actions, and new patterns for relationships. At conversion God changes the old motivations for action to a new one. Believers seek God. They value His will, and they have an innate desire for holiness. While this desire can be distorted and diminished by sin, it cannot be eradicated. This truth explains why there is often frustration in a Christian's life.

In our description of old person/new person, we have presented the truth that Christians struggle with sin. That does not mean that they struggle with the question of whether or not they want to sin. That question is settled at conversion. Christians do not want to sin, but the inner struggle may continue to bring tension to their daily walk.

I do not understand what I do.
For what I want to do I do not
do, but what I hate I do.
Romans 7:15

The struggle is intense. Paul presented two parallels from two different perspectives—the law and his own nature. But he never described the struggle as between two natures. The problem was a struggle between what he knew to do and the flesh that would not do it (see Rom. 7:14-25). This struggle is also described in Galatians 5:16-18 where the Spirit and the flesh oppose each other.

For our purposes we should note two points. First, this text teaches nothing about two natures. The struggle consists of the failure to accomplish the transformation the mind desires. The Christian struggles to become better. Second, the struggle indicates a frustration factor. Frustration comes from the inability to live up to the knowledge we possess.

These passages explain a basic life component. When we fail to live up to what we know to do, we will be frustrated. To the degree that our lives fail to conform to the insights of the mind, there will frustration too. The solution is Jesus Christ. He alone brings desire and performance into harmony. On the other hand, when we live up to our expectations, we experience peace. In fact, any improvement in living as we know we should brings peace. Still, without help, none of us can bring actual improvement in line with expectations.

CONCLUSION

The point of this chapter may be illustrated by the different phases of a man's life. When men are not married, we call them bachelors. When a bachelor chooses a woman to be his wife, usually there is an engagement period. During that time he is still a bachelor, but even then there are indications his life is about to change—radically. During the wedding the bachelor promises himself to the woman, and the pastor pronounces them husband and wife. In an instant his situation changed. He is no longer a *bachelor*; he is a *husband*.

In his vows he promised to be a husband, and both he and his wife hoped he'd be a good one. Still, sometimes problems arise in a relationship. Some husbands never quite grasp the concept. They continue to live as if their own interests and needs are primary. Perhaps they continue going out with the guys. Perhaps they spend all their money on themselves. Some even run around with other women, disregarding their vows to purity and monogamy. People may react by saying: "Doesn't he know he has a wife?" "Doesn't he know he made promises?" "Doesn't he know he is no longer a bachelor?"

This last question targets the problem. Regardless of how the husband lives after his marriage, he is no longer a bachelor. The solution is to realize and accept who he really is, a husband, and get on with that part of his life. Further, the more he fails to act like a husband, the more frustrated he will become. Everywhere he goes and no matter what he does, he has a voice inside reminding him he is not keeping the commitment he made. In other words, a married man cannot act like a bachelor and be happy in it.

When individuals come to Christ, it is similar to a wedding. In a single moment, promises are made which affect those persons the rest of their lives. Once Christians are converted, they become new persons. No matter what they do or

Once Christians are converted, they become new persons.

Failure to achieve victory over sin is the result of living inappropriately.

how they live, they will always be the new person. Continuing the analogy, when a Christian disobeys Christ, it's similar to the husband who continues to live like a bachelor. The relationship with Christ is affected when Christians live disobedient lives. Even though their hearts may be deeply committed to the things of God, they will not experience the joy of salvation and will carry guilt and frustration into every aspect of their lives. Failure to achieve victory over sin is the result of living inappropriately. Christians cannot say, "that was my old person."

The point of this chapter is very simple. At the time of conversion you are *changed*. You are *regenerated*. You are *responsible* for your life and your relationship with Christ. You cannot blame failure on anyone else, including a bad nature. If all the proper ingredients are in place, in time you should mature and become a successful Christian. Chapter 4 reveals the proper ingredients for growth.

PERSONAL LEARNING ACTIVITY

Answer each of the following questions by indicating (Y) Yes or (N) No.

___ **Have you received Christ and experienced conversion?**

___ **Have you accepted responsibility for your life in Christ?**

___ **Are you growing in your relationship to God through Jesus Christ?**

___ **Do you sometimes blame failure as a Christian on someone else?**

___ **Are you steadily becoming a mature and successful Christian?**

CHAPTER 4

WHAT'S NEW ABOUT A CHRISTIAN?

One day I had lunch with Gary. Gary was a very successful businessman. He had been employed at the same major corporation since graduating from college approximately 25 years earlier. They were good to him, and he exemplified the company's values. He advanced rapidly through the ranks including time spent in many of their plants and working in the main office. At this point in time he worked directly under the president. Now Gary was having problems at work. Things at the office were pretty much the same–but Gary wasn't. In the middle of his career he had become a Christian. He grew rapidly in his faith and was delighted that his corporation operated based on values which were consistent with his newfound faith.

Eventually another corporate group with different values purchased Gary's company. He had increasing difficulty with the new corporate ethics and practices. While the company continued to affirm him and advanced him beyond his peers, Gary was restless. His long hours affected his family. He found less time to be involved in church activities, and his energy was sapped. In addition, Gary did not agree with some of the company's new contractual relationships. He felt increasing concern for the promotion of their products in a politically repressive country. Gary needed a change.

Many Christians experience similar situations. Frequently Christians' personal lives and corporate lives collide. Like Gary, their situations call for difficult decisions. On the one hand security, salary, and solid relationships may continue for years to come. On the other, matters of conscience relentlessly plague their thoughts and dampen enthusiasm for all of life. Conversion brings conviction. The new person differs from the old person. Certainly the difference is felt, but what actually *is* different? At least three areas of life feel the change from old to new: values, ambitions, and pleasures.

VALUES OF THE CHRISTIAN LIFE

When we value God, we will include Him in every aspect of our lives.

Values are the things we most prize—the things we hold most dear. Values motivate us to achievement. They also help us to measure personal success. When we value health, we will take care of our bodies. When we value family, we will be our best for our spouses, children, and extended family. When we value God, we will include Him in every aspect of our lives. Our values are foundational to life, the platform supporting our ambitions and pleasures.

At conversion our values change. The conflict over values helps explain why it often takes months for people to accept Christ if they do not have a Christian background. They have to embrace a different worldview and choose to accept Christ.

The Bible contains many passages that speak to the change of values. One such passage is 2 Corinthians 5:17. In an earlier chapter we discussed how all things become new at conversion. In the surrounding context Paul clarified the issues involved; two are identified in verses 15 and 16. In verse 15, Paul revealed that Christians have an obligation to live for the Christ who died for them. Christians value living for Christ because they have discovered real life in Him. In verse 16, Paul explained one of the major differences in perspective between non-Christians and Christians. Referring to his own experience, he disclosed that previously he had measured both Christ and people "from a worldly point of view." Literally the Greek language says "according to the flesh" which means that Paul evaluated people in a normal, natural way. Valuing things in the natural way causes us to make artificial appraisals of people based on such things as race, religion, and economic situation. This is the way we look at the world and appraise people when we consider ourselves the center of life.

Paul also viewed Christ through the lens of a natural perspective. No doubt this impacted his attempts to cleanse the world of Christians and of any trace of Jesus. As a rabbi and probably a member of the Sanhedrin, Paul agreed with those who found Jesus guilty of blasphemy. He perceived Him to be a troublemaker. Viewing Jesus "according to the flesh" meant that he could not receive God's evaluation of Jesus nor could he grasp that Jesus was God's Messiah.

A relationship with Christ changes that. Paul explained in verse 16 that his values changed that perspective. As a Christian he valued Christ according to the spirit. He also viewed humanity differently. Paul's understanding of the value of people now came from the Spirit.

Since 2 Corinthians 5:17 says all things are new, conversion brings a comprehensive change in a Christian's outlook. Our worldview and value system revolve around three points. We are naturally prone to put ourselves first. Second, we live in a context of time, locked into history and movement. We cannot embrace qualities that do not have roots in time. Yet as Christians we must value eternity. Third, we seek our own comfort. Therefore things that make life safe, secure, easier, or more fun have value. If anyone touches our things or possessions, they touch us deeply.

Therefore, if anyone is in Christ, he is a new creation; the old has gone, the new has come!
2 Corinthians 5:17

These values may not be comprehensive, but they are definitely representative of the core. Holiness means living by God's value system rather than our own, accepting God's patterns for life rather than the world's. The following discussion illustrates how values change when we meet Christ.

GOD OVER SELF

The most radical and core change in a believer is a movement from egocentricity to the centrality of God. Everything changes. Many passages affirm this core change.

The Gospels include a variety of references to the need to put God first in our lives. In Luke 14:33, Jesus explained the cost of discipleship. He said, "Any of you who does not give up everything he has cannot be my disciple." That statement, when taken at face value, is radical; but it is consistent with the teaching He developed in that context. In verse 26 He identified potential barriers to following Christ: father and mother, brother and sister, wife and children, and one's own life. No doubt these seemed harsh words to those listening. In this instance, Jesus' point was that a person who loves his family more than he loves God cannot participate in God's kingdom. Family values can be properly appreciated when loving God and following Christ comes first.

Family values can be properly appreciated when loving God and following Christ comes first.

In writing to the church at Philippi, the apostle Paul explained his own pilgrimage (see Phil. 3:4-14) to counter those who built their lives on the world's value system. Paul's background was impeccable. He identified his heredity (see v. 5), and what he had attained through his own achievements (see vv. 5-6). No one could fault either. Yet they had led him down the wrong path. His ambitions did not include Christ.

At conversion Paul's values changed radically. Verses 7 and 8 explained the change. Paul reached a point where he considered these things hindrances to gaining Christ. He used a Greek expression showing purpose, "in order that," to demonstrate that he gave up one to gain the other. Neither heredity nor achievement is necessarily wrong. The problem was that Paul trusted in them instead of Christ. Once converted, however, the greatest value in his life was knowing Christ (see v. 10).

When we are saved, God becomes more important than anything else in our lives—even more important than life itself. This change in values evidences itself in the desire to know Christ, to be like Christ, and to be with Christ. The practical outworking of this is revealed in a life that grows progressively more holy and more renewed in the image of its Creator. Millions of Christians have testified that they have experienced greater joy and self-fulfillment in placing Christ first in their lives and submitting to the lordship of Jesus.

PERSONAL LEARNING ACTIVITY

Many Christians have found a greater joy and self-fulfillment in placing Christ first in their lives. If this is your testimony, write a short paragraph explaining why this is so.

_____

_____

If you have struggled with the issue of placing Christ first in your life, what keeps you from making that commitment?

_____

_____

ETERNITY OVER TIME

God calls us to consider the priority of things that are eternal over things that are temporal. The second area of changing values at conversion is eternity over time. This means seeking His kingdom instead of seeking the things of this world.

Philosophers have long debated whether there is an afterlife, and if so, what it is like. The secular conclusions of the 20th century lead us to one of two positions. First, there is no after-

God calls us to consider the priority of things that are eternal over things that are temporal.

life. Second, we cannot know about the afterlife so we should live for the present. Both of these conclusions have led to a focus on here and now as opposed to then and there. Merchandisers popularize these conclusions. They have convinced our world that this life and its values are all we really know; therefore we should "grab all the gusto" while we can. They encourage us to make the most of this life since, from their perspective, anything else is highly unlikely. Increasingly in our modern society, few have a perspective beyond time.

The root of this secular perspective is an anti-God bias. The basic questions are whether there is a God and, if so, whether we can know Him. While most people believe that God must exist, some philosophers have reached radically different conclusions. Because of their conclusions, people who live for eternity rather than time are perceived as bizarre or odd. Yet the Bible continually warns us that there is an afterlife and a judgment to follow (see Heb. 9:27). Further, it teaches that we cannot live this life properly unless we can solve the problem of death and the afterlife (see Heb. 2:15). Therefore, the change of focus from time to eternity is a necessary step in achieving holiness.

The change of focus from time to eternity is a necessary step in achieving holiness.

Many of Jesus' parables emphasized this truth. For example, in Luke 12:13-21, Jesus told the parable of the rich fool. The man prospered in his business, so he decided to tear down his barns and build bigger ones. He desired the security that material possessions provide. But he took no thought for spiritual security. Then the man died and entered a world for which he was totally unprepared—the afterlife. In conclusion Jesus said, "This is how it will be with anyone who stores up things for himself but is not rich toward God" (v. 21).

Jesus illustrated the truth even more graphically when He told the parable of the shrewd manager (see Luke 16:1-15). The manager was warned that he would lose his job for improper management. The man reduced the debt of the master's creditors. His rationale was that they would appreciate him and when he had no job, at least he would have friends. In the story the master commended the manager for his shrewdness, but when we read the parable today, we struggle with what appears to be an unethical situation. Yet Jesus acknowledged the dishonesty of the manager and did not commend him for his dishonest actions. The point of the story occurs elsewhere. Jesus summarized the parable by challenging His disciples to "use worldly wealth" to gain entrance "into eternal dwellings" (v. 9). The story contrasts the values of time with eternity. Jesus wanted the disciples— and us—to realize that one day we, too, will lose the security that earth affords. Since that time is inevitable, we would be wise to use the assets of time to prepare for eternity.

The Epistles also contain repeated examples of this point. The apostle Paul spoke exactly to this issue. People who opposed his ministry questioned him about his life and his call to serve God. Paul answered them in 2 Corinthians 4:7-18. He made constant references to the persecutions and hardships he endured for the sake of bringing the gospel to them (see vv. 7-12). He spoke of his own decaying body contrasted with the growth of his inner spirit (see vv. 16-17). Paul expressed his motivation in verses 17 and 18: "For our light and momentary troubles are achieving for us an eternal glory that far outweighs them all. So we fix our eyes not on what is seen, but on what is unseen. For what is seen is temporary, but what is unseen is eternal." This passage compares eternity to our physical well-being. One of our greatest values is health. Even so, living for eternity is more important than maintaining health on earth.

The apostle James warned his readers about a preoccupation with the values of earth instead of the values of heaven. He envisioned a group of businessmen making plans for the expansion of their business (see Jas. 4:13-17). Their basic problem was the assumption that life would go on, and that they must make a living while they could. James also warned of an arrogant life plan that disregards God and then offered a corrective: "Instead, you ought to say, 'if it is the Lord's will, we will live and do this or that'" (v. 15). Once again the Bible commends a worldview that considers eternity more important than time or success on earth.

At this point it's easy to move to the opposite extreme. Many Christians so live for eternity that they have neglected their responsibilities in time. They have assumed God would take care of responsibilities He has delegated to them. Not so. The Bible commends a balanced life. In fact, we are instructed to take care of family, health, and work responsibilities. However, none of these things are as important as preparing for eternity. God urges us to be realistic about life. Since He created us as eternal beings, life includes time but, more importantly, it includes eternity. A wise person orchestrates the affairs of life to include God.

PEOPLE OVER THINGS

The third area revealing the change in value systems at conversion is the value of people over things. This is radically different from the world's perspective. Our world values people as long as they do not interfere with personal goals and security—the exact opposite of God's value system.

Once again, this change is illustrated in the Gospels and the Epistles. One day Jesus encountered a young man of wealth and position (see Luke 18:18-30). To the man's credit he also had spiritual interests. He wanted to enter the kingdom of God, so he inquired of Jesus about it. What could he do? Jesus' words pierced to the heart of the problem: "Go and sell everything you have and give to the poor" (v. 22). Jesus put his finger on the man's basic problem. The man loved his wealth more than he loved God. A second issue also presented itself. The man loved his money more than he loved people. In his refusal to do what Jesus instructed, the man revealed he had the same problem with both God and people. His values were wrong.

Jesus did not require everyone who inquired about entrance to the kingdom to sell everything he owned. Nevertheless, in every person there is something difficult to release—even for God's kingdom. The numerous passages in which Jesus urged His followers to consider the poor reveal one of the basic kingdom values. God cares more for people than He does for things. Jesus demonstrated this in leaving heaven to come to earth to die for people. Christians will embrace the same values.

Once again we observe this value in the apostle Paul. In 1 Corinthians 9, he defended his rights as an apostle to the church at Corinth. But rather than focus on rights, Paul focused his thoughts on responsibilities. Even though he had a right to a wife and support from the church, he did without both (see vv. 3-14). He knew that financial gain could interfere with his ministry. He also knew that marriage would be unwise for him because of his ministry responsibilities. The apostle Paul clearly understood that people are more important than money and personal privileges.

These examples illustrate the changed value system that occurs at conversion. Most Christians do not realize that following Christ will radically change their lives. Generally we come to Christ out of need, hoping He will meet us and deliver us from our immediate concerns. Regardless of what prompts our movement to accept Christ, no one moves to Him without a sense of personal weakness—and therefore failure. Along with failure is a willingness to change our ways to His. We believe He will give us better than we have—and God does just that.

Not all Christians live in accord with God's values. However, from the moment we come to Christ, the Spirit of God urges people to accept these new attitudes. Frustration builds, in part, because the Holy Spirit directs His energy toward effecting these changes in us, and we do not always willingly embrace them. That frustration is relieved when we live in

God cares more for people than He does for things— a basic kingdom value.

harmony with the Holy Spirit and His leadership. The bottom line is that salvation brings a new value system. God expects us to accept His values. When we do, there is spiritual success. At the heart of His value system are the truths that God is more important than self, eternity is more important than time, and people are more important than things.

PERSONAL LEARNING ACTIVITY

The above section states that God is more important than self, eternity is more important than time, and people are more important than things. Is this your value system? ❑ Yes ❑ No

How are you growing in your understanding and application of these values?

_____

_____

AMBITIONS OF THE CHRISTIAN LIFE

At conversion God changes our hearts so that we possess new ambitions. Ambitions are internal actions/movements to achieve what we value. Viewing one's personal ambitions may reveal whether one is living as a Christian or non-Christian. The values of God, eternity, and people motivate us to a different lifestyle than the values of self and things.

> **The values of God, eternity, and people motivate us to a different lifestyle than the values of self and things.**

Scripture reveals at least five ambitions that characterize mature Christians. Not all Christians live by these ambitions, but they are what God intends and the Holy Spirit seeks to encourage them in us. As we respond to the Spirit's leading, we will devote our energies to success in the following activities: worship, Christian lifestyle, stewardship, ministry, and family relationships.

WORSHIP

Worship is at the heart of all Christian activity. Worship means to appreciate God for who He is and to enjoy Him for what He does. Jesus taught us how to worship. In His encounter with the Samaritan woman at the well, He spoke of worship (see John 4:1-42). One of the issues which separated the Jews from the Samaritans was the place of worship. Jews worshiped at the Jerusalem temple while Samaritans worshiped at the Samaritan temple. Jesus explained that with His coming He brought a new dimension to worship. Up until that time, the place of worship *was* important. With His coming, the spirit rather than the place of worship became primary. He taught, "True worshipers will worship the Father in spirit and truth, for they are the kind of worshipers the Father seeks" (v. 23).

> **Worship means to appreciate God for who He is and to enjoy Him for what He does.**

Worship in spirit and truth demands the involvement of the entire person. It calls for consistency of word and action and the total commitment of every facet of the person to God. Since the Father seeks worshipers, putting God before self means, in part, that we fill the mind with worship of God, communicating with Him in spirit and truth. Pure and effective worship is one of the high ambitions of the believer.

CHRISTIAN LIFESTYLE

The ambition to live a consistent Christian lifestyle grows out of new values. The complexities of translating theology into proper everyday living is a challenge. In fact, much of the New Testament, especially Paul's epistles, addresses that very issue. The Epistles are corrective in nature (see 1 Cor. 5:9-11, referring to a letter written prior to 1 Corinthians; also Gal. 1:6-9, for example). Other Letters, however, respond to questions of how to be what God intends. For example, 1 Corinthians is written in response to a visit from Christians at Corinth who reported their situation and asked questions raised from the congregation regarding clarification of theological issues (see 1 Cor. 7:1). Christian lifestyle is the subject of most of the New Testament and a major reason for writing it, but some specific passages help to reinforce the point.

Jesus anticipated the issue when He delivered His famous Sermon on the Mount (see Matt. 5–7). Much of the sermon discusses proper attitudes and relationships for Christians. For practical, everyday living the central passage is 6:25-34. In this passage Jesus addressed the issues of food and health (see v. 25), clothes (see v. 28), and life itself (see vv. 27,34). These things cause people to worry, and they reveal a major difference between God's people and non-Christians (see vv. 32-33).

Seek first his kingdom and his righteousness, and all these things will be given to you as well.
Matthew 6:33

Two directives provide instruction for the Christian. Both are taught or implied in Matthew 6:33. First, God's people should seek His kingdom as a priority. This restates the new value of God over self. Rather than the concerns that occupy our thoughts and energy as non-Christians, we are to devote our lives and energies to God's concerns. A Christian's primary concern is God's kingdom and personal righteousness (see v. 33). Second, God's people should trust God for His provision. Jesus contrasted the frantic activity of pagans (they "run after all these things") with the quiet assurance of Christians ("your heavenly Father knows," v. 32). His words speak to the lifestyle of His people. We trust God for life and the provisions of life and place more priority on the kingdom of God than personal concerns.

These themes occur repeatedly in the Epistles as well. In responding to specific life issues, the writers addressed personal commitment to God's will as well as trusting God for life's needs. Regarding the first, Paul often urged Christians to develop Christian purity and character. For example, sanctification is the will of God (see 1 Thess. 4:3), Christians are "to live a life worthy of the calling" (Eph. 4:1), we are to have "the mind of Christ" (Phil. 2:5), and we are to set our hearts and minds on things above rather than things on earth (see Phil. 3:12-14). Other New Testament writers presented the same theme. The writer of Hebrews urged his readers on to Christian "maturity" (6:1), to approach God with genuineness, purity, faith, and hope (see 10:19-25), "and to be holy" (12:14). James reminded his readers of the need for displaying wisdom in good deeds (see 3:13) and of the necessity of clean hands and pure hearts (see 4:8). Peter called his readers to holiness as God "is holy" (1 Pet. 1:15), to clean and pure lives (see 1 Pet. 2:11-12), and "to escape the corruption in the world" (2 Pet. 1:4). The apostle John writing near the end of his life observed second- and third-generation Christians and encouraged them to overcome sin (see 1 John 2:1), to keep God's commandments (see 1 John 2:3), to overcome the world (see 1 John 2:15-17; 4:4), and to imitate "what is good" (3 John 11).

STEWARDSHIP

The third illustration of the new ambitions characterizing a Christian is stewardship. Biblical stewardship is an issue of life—not just money. God wants us to use all we have and are for His purposes. As we seek to live consistently, we develop a strong sense of stewardship for everything God has provided. God gives us all things, and the situations of life provide opportunities to be what and where God intends. Each of us represents God in our own unique way.

Biblical stewardship is an issue of life—not just money.

Several stewardship qualities emerge in 2 Corinthians 8. First, stewardship was the result of a grace from God. This principle incorporates two ideas: that God brought them the grace of conversion, and that as they lived out their response to grace, God continued to impress upon them the opportunity of giving. Giving was a matter of God's grace (see v. 1). Another of the qualities of stewardship was the matter of joy. Their joy was in responding to God's will and sharing with others in need. Even though they were in very difficult situations of poverty, their joy was to give. Poverty did not keep them from accomplishing what God desired for their lives (see v. 2). Also, they considered their gifts to be fellowship with other Christians. They under-

81

stood well the interconnectedness of Christians as brothers and sisters. The Macedonian stewardship extended to others because of the privilege of sharing in their hardships (see v. 4). Finally, this was an outworking of devotion. These churches were committed first to the Lord and second to the apostle Paul (see v. 5). Stewardship of life is a natural outworking of a deep commitment to God, one of the Christian's new ambitions.

MINISTRY

Ministry is the fourth ambition expressing new values. When we have met Christ, ministry becomes a priority and can take many forms. Not every Christian ministers the same because of the Holy Spirit's gifts. Even so, every obedient Christian will have a desire to minister to others. This clearly emphasizes the value of people over things.

Jesus set a high example of self-giving service. He indicated that He came for the purpose of serving others, and that His followers must be servants as well (see Mark 10:43-45). His greatest illustration occurred the night before His crucifixion. In the upper room Jesus commanded His disciples to be like Him—a servant (see John 13:13-16).

The Epistles reinforce the ministry norm for Christians. Paul stated it of himself on several occasions (see Phil. 2:17). He also advocated the priority of love for others (see Rom. 12: 9-10; 13:8-10), not returning evil when evil is done to you (see Rom. 12:17-21) and serving the Lord and the church through exercising the gifts of the Spirit (see 1 Cor. 12:27-31).

The Holy Spirit equips and directs us so that we are able to maximize our contributions to the kingdom as well as represent Christ to the unsaved world.

The Holy Spirit urges Christians toward ministry. He equips and directs us so that we are able to maximize our contribution to the kingdom as well as represent Christ to the unsaved world. One of the new ambitions following conversion is to minister to others. Ministry is an outworking of the "people over things" value system in a new Christian.

FAMILY RELATIONSHIPS

The final illustration of new ambitions is a renewed interest in the family. Christians soon learn that God has a plan for the family. God ordained the family—husband, wife, and children. He established clear guidelines for family organization and relationships. Spiritual interest for the family begins at conversion and often one family member is instrumental in leading others to Christ.

One of the natural outworkings of salvation is a desire for the family to be what God intended when He established it originally in the garden of Eden. The family is God's way to nurture, respect, and rear children. It provides for emotionally well-rounded persons, for the deepest levels of social interaction, and for a conducive environment to nurture the maturing process.

There is a deeper dimension, however. God had a purpose beyond what we can see. God desires that the family be like Him. It should be the closest place to heaven on earth. The family's complex human relationships should portray the complex divine relationships among the Trinity. Since God exists as three-in-one, He understands the multiple relationships and communication problems faced in community. Yet He perfectly loves and perfectly communicates. He also functions in perfect harmony to achieve the divine tasks even though they are divided among the persons of the Trinity. The family should emulate God's relationships, His effective communication, and His ability to function well.

The family should emulate God's relationships, His effective communication, and His ability to function well.

Accomplishing this is a growth process. In a properly functioning family, people learn how to relate to one another from a secure environment and with proper, personal self-understanding. Family members also learn spiritual truths that can be learned only from sustaining the close relationships demanded in family life. God is revealed in the family since it is the place where the most intimate of relationships occurs. Individual family members see one another's imperfections, as well as their own, and they rejoice in the growth of others. Further, the family represents God to the world. Just as husband and wife are to picture the Christ/church relationship (see Eph. 5:28-32), the family is to be a picture of the Godhead. When others observe the Christian family, they should be impressed with their love for one another as well as the supporting spiritual dynamic.

The Christian family is a powerful witness to the world.

The point is that the Holy Spirit encourages us to develop the ambition of having properly functioning, spiritually powerful families. This occurs as a result of time spent together developing common interests and goals as well as time spent together in prayer, Bible study, and ministry. This empowers us to experience the joy of fellowship at the deepest of human relationships and is heightened by the presence of the Lord Himself. The Christian family is a powerful witness to the world and one of the highest and most personally rewarding of all goals and ambitions.

PERSONAL LEARNING ACTIVITY

Review the previous section, focusing on New Ambitions. On the continuum below, using the first letter of each area, indicate how much you have grown in these areas as you have sought to live for and follow Christ.

Worship; Christian Lifestyle; Stewardship; Ministry; Family Relationships

Little	Moderate	Much

PLEASURES OF THE CHRISTIAN LIFE

So far we have discussed two of the three changes that occur when one is saved. First, God changes a person so that there are new values. Second, the new values lead to new ambitions. Now let's explore the third change—new pleasures. Pleasures are the things we enjoy. Generally our pleasures grow from our ambitions. The more we are able to achieve our ambitions, the more pleasure we derive from a particular activity or event. For example, if being in good physical shape is a value and a regular exercise program is an ambition, pleasure comes when we live according to that value and ambition. We derive satisfaction and joy, not to mention a myriad of other benefits.

For those who are more sedate, perhaps the following illustration is applicable. If one of our values is the proper-functioning family, an ambition is to actively seek and promote God's will in our families. As we achieve this ambition, there is pleasure. It is most satisfying and enjoyable for a parent or grandparent to observe as their grandchildren choose spiritual values or make proper, God-honoring choices in life's many complex situations.

Pleasures bring satisfaction to the degree that they build on proper values and ambitions. If the basic value is wrong because it is too short-lived or unwisely chosen, then the effort to achieve will be misspent. Any pleasure experienced will also be short-lived, since, like the value on which it is based, it is temporary. That is why Scripture constantly instructs us to build our lives on a solid foundation—*the* solid foundation. Jesus contrasted the foolish and wise men who build their houses on sand and rock, respectively (see Matt. 7:24-27). Paul exhorted Christians to live so that they would receive appropriate rewards in heaven (see 1 Cor. 3:12-15). Though the words have primary reference to the work of Christian ministers who build on Christ as the only proper foundation, the implication is that all Christians will give account for their life's effort.

> **Pleasures bring satisfaction to the degree that they build on proper values and ambitions.**

The Scriptures provide a strong indication about which pleasures bring lasting satisfaction. Psalm 1 praises the person whose "delight is in the law of God" (v. 2). God's Word brings pleasure because it can guide us into the lasting joys of life. In Colossians 3:1-2, Paul spoke of the lordship of Jesus as bringing the maximum good. He used two synonyms to express it. These are translated as "set your hearts on things above," and "set your minds on things above." They remind us that our successes and joys come from having a deep desire for and involvement with activities/possessions that honor Jesus. In expressing his own new ambitions, Paul spoke of an ongoing goal in life that brought him lasting satisfaction. He said in Philippians 3:8-11 that his new, all-consuming goal was "to know Christ." Every facet of Paul's experience could be related to knowing Jesus well and attaining the joy of the resurrection from the dead.

As Christians walk with God and become more like Him, their pleasures change. They derive increasing satisfaction from achieving success related to the direction imposed by their new values.

CONCLUSION

Every aspect of life becomes different when Jesus is Lord.

What is distinctively different at conversion is a new spiritual interest and direction. As stated earlier, not every Christian immediately realizes the changes. But regeneration brings a new openness to God, and the Holy Spirit brings new insights and motivations. Life is lived with sensitivity to God, eternity, and other people. This leads to spiritual ambitions in worship, ministry, Christian living, stewardship, and family relationships. Sometimes people separate their lives into sacred and secular and live with a compartmentalization that segregates their Christian faith from many aspects of life. They wonder what interest God has in work, recreation, financial security, or other "secular" activities. But such compartmentalization fails to grasp the fact that God saves the entire person. Every aspect of life becomes different when Jesus is Lord. Why? Because He is Lord of all. Even the more routine demands of the past are energized with new responsibility and power.

How does this relate to our discussion of holiness? As we mature in Christ, we will become more like Him. The values, ambitions, and pleasures of the old person will be replaced by the values, ambitions, and pleasures of the new person. This does not occur overnight. But we should have an awareness of what the Holy Spirit intends in our lifestyles. His working seems "intuitional" for the believer.

This chapter also focused on principles, not specific activities. It is impossible to provide a list of *what to do when*. Even if such a list could be provided, that is not God's intent. God intends for His people to understand the principles of their new life and from that understanding be able to respond to the issues that present themselves at any time or in any situation. Sanctification is a process of growth as two personalities interact. God relates to us personally, leading us along in ways that are appropriate to His will and our abilities. It is our privilege to live out the principles and become holy.

So far we have discussed what holiness is and what happens at conversion. The discussion provides information about Christian living and gives incentive for personal growth. But knowing these things will not make us holy; more is required. The remaining chapters discuss how to live successfully. In living as God intends, we will become holy and, as a result, happy.

PERSONAL LEARNING ACTIVITY
**In the margin list the possessions/people/
activities/achievements in your life that are
extremely important to you. Now circle the
ones which are connected with growth in
Christ and your quest for holiness.**

CHAPTER 5

EFFECTING CHANGE

In 1864 President Abraham Lincoln issued his Emancipation Proclamation. The historic document proclaimed freedom for slaves in America. The Emancipation Proclamation served to rally the North and hasten the end of the war as well as the terrible practice of human slavery in the United States. The proclamation was great news, but many questions remained. The war was still being fought, and Confederate troops still occupied many areas in the South. The basic question for a slave who heard the proclamation was, "Am I really free?"

At conversion God says we are holy, free from sin, and able to have complete fellowship with Him. Yet there is a major difference between being declared holy–free from sin's power in life–and actually being holy. The new Christian has made a choice to side with God over evil, and, perhaps for the first time, has entered the battle of the ages. There are spiritual attacks from the outside, and there are habits, fears, lusts, and pressures on the inside. The question for Christians is, "Am I really holy?"

The slaves of 1864 were legally free. But what would it take for slaves to actually be free? There were three essential steps to realizing that freedom. They are the same steps for realizing holiness in the believer's life.

First, the slaves would have to possess the knowledge that the Emancipation Proclamation provided freedom. Without knowledge of the proclamation, slaves could live in slavery indefinitely. *Second,* slaves would have to make difficult choices. The choices involved decisions they had never been allowed to make. They did not know how to live as free people, nor did they have the necessary resources to begin living a life of freedom. The first crucial step was to "choose" to gather their belongings and families, exercise the newly promised freedom to walk away from the plantation, and choose a new life. *Third,* slaves would have to have power. The former slaves faced the power exerted by the masters to keep them as slaves. Other slave owners and the entire army of the south could force them back to their masters. To achieve real freedom, the slaves needed resources beyond themselves.

Similarly, Christians must have the power to be able to effect the choices they make in their quest for holiness. This chapter explores the three basic issues confronting Christians in their daily battles for holiness: knowledge, choices, and power.

KNOWLEDGE

The basic foundation for change is knowledge. God works primarily in and through the mind. Almost all Christian growth begins with some understanding of certain issues, life patterns, and possibilities. Once the mind is confident, it is able to influence the rest of the person to choose what is right.

The basic foundation for change is knowledge.

THE MIND IN THE NEW TESTAMENT

Scripture frequently addresses the significance of the mind in personal transformation. The Greek word for *mind* is *noos* and occurs 24 times in the New Testament, 12 of which are in the Pauline Epistles. The word may therefore be considered a Pauline distinctive. Certainly Paul's discussion fits the general tenor of Scripture that people live as their minds instruct. Sometimes the word conveys the meaning of *understanding,* "the faculty of being able to think." In this sense Paul was able to say that he would rather not speak in tongues because in so doing the "mind is unfruitful" (1 Cor. 14:14). It is better to use the mind in

And the peace of God, which transcends all understanding, will guard your hearts and your minds in Christ Jesus.
Philippians 4:7

worshiping God. He warned of being shaken in the mind because of a misunderstanding of theology (see 2 Thess. 2:2). Further, Paul indicated that God's peace surpasses the ability to think through specific fears (see Phil. 4:7). Paul warned of Gentiles whom God has allowed to pursue depraved or reprobate thoughts (see Rom. 1:28). One characteristic of persons without Christ is that they use their minds for things other than the interests of God (see Eph. 4:17; Col. 2:18). Consequently, they have depraved and unclean minds (see 2 Tim. 3:8; Titus 1:15). Christians can have uncertainty and even ambivalence in their minds (see Rom. 14:5). One of God's major works in conversion is to "change the mind" so that people embrace God's truth.

Discussions of depravity often confuse us. In everyday conversations we speak of the depraved as those who commit the most hideous and extreme sins. But in the Bible the word is not used with such restricted meaning. The Bible uses the term *depraved* to mean "cut off from God." The depraved mind does not have the light of God's Holy Spirit within and, therefore, centers all the issues of life around itself. It describes the blindness sin produces in all of us that leads to sinful actions. Even unsaved people can do good things because of the inner impulse that comes from being created in the image of God. Moral people are quite capable of deriving appropriate standards of living. When they reason together with others who seek to live consistently moral lives, they clarify and accept even higher standards (see Rom. 2:1-16). In Romans 2:17-29, Paul discussed the situation of religious people; he used the Jewish heritage as the prime example. Some unsaved people own a Bible, read it, and value it. The issue for them is whether they live up to it.

Paul acknowledged that at times people can and do choose to live correctly. Since they do make correct choices on occasion, they possess enough knowledge to value proper choices and good moral conduct. Yet being able to recognize and value moral and religious conduct makes us responsible to live consistently moral and religious lives. When we fail to live up to these standards, we reveal that we are candidates for God's judgment.

Paul summarized his discussion on the need for salvation in Romans 3:9-20. Using multiple Old Testament texts to prove his point, he explained that no one does good, no one seeks God, and all people are self-centered. This is the biblical meaning of depravity. Depravity is living without regard to God's will for our lives. All people naturally live that way. Because of that, we know the mind is corrupt and depraved.

Depravity is living without regard to God's will for our lives.

Perhaps the central passage devoted to the importance of the mind is Romans 12:1-2. After presenting Scripture's most theologically precise discussion of salvation, the apostle Paul turned his thoughts to practical matters of Christian living. He stated:

> *Therefore, I urge you, brothers, in view of God's mercy, to offer your bodies as living sacrifices, holy and pleasing to God–this is your spiritual act of worship. Do not conform any longer to the pattern of this world, but be transformed by the renewing of your mind. Then you will be able to test and approve what God's will is–his good, pleasing and perfect will.*

The terms *offer, sacrifices, holy and pleasing to God,* and *act of worship* come from the sacrificial language and imagery of Israel. This passage speaks directly to the point of personal holiness–being separated to God.

The relationship between mind and body is of primary importance for this study. To be more precise, Paul contrasted the two suggesting that he conceived of the body as the mind's implementer. The body does what the mind thinks. Paul anticipated this in Romans 6:11-14 where he urged his readers to present their members (body parts and human characteristics) to God to avoid the body's being used for evil.

It is clear that our minds are the instruments for control of our bodies. Romans 12:1-2 explains that offering the body to the Lord includes the mind but also reveals the tension described so many times in this book. We are to present our bodies as "holy and pleasing to God" (v. 1). This verse refers to the initial act of separating ourselves to God for His purposes. But actual holiness requires more than making a climactic commitment to God. What was previously unholy must become holy. There must be a personal transformation and that occurs in the "renewing of the mind."

A metamorphosis is a change of form that begins inside and works its way out.

The words of this text are picturesque. The first picture is of a mold or form. The unbeliever lives in a constant pattern of conformity. The world shapes everyone into a mold. The shaping comes from external pressures of the environment, but it also comes from personal participation in the world's values and activities (see Jas. 1:13-15). We naturally and willingly participate in the world's values because of its affinity with our minds. The second picture is of a metamorphosis. The believer can be "transformed." The literal picture is of a butterfly undergoing a metamorphosis. A metamorphosis is a change of form that begins inside and works its way out. In contrast to the external pressures which squeeze one into conformity with the world, if the mind is changed it has the capacity to change the entire person. Thus, there is a change from within (the mind) working its way out (the body).

The actual transformation of the person is proportionate to the renewing of the mind. The mind does not change immediately. There are habits that take time to change. The mind must understand and embrace the needed changes as well as grasp a plan for making them. At conversion God begins the process of renewal. This renewal process is the same as discussed previously in connection with the "old person/new person" theology. Some illustrative passages will help to explain how the Bible provides the knowledge and the manner in which the mind must change.

═══════════════ ❧✟❧ ═══════════════

PERSONAL LEARNING ACTIVITY

**Reread Romans 12:1-2. In what ways do you
identify with the phrases "offer your bodies
as living sacrifices," "holy and pleasing to
God," and "spiritual act of worship."**

_____

_____

**In what ways do you identify with "Do not
conform any longer to the pattern of this
world" and "be transformed by the renewing
of your mind"?**

_____

_____

CONTRASTING WAYS OF LIFE

One way of helping the mind grasp the things of God is to contrast God's will and the world's way. Many texts illustrate this with specific issues of life that make the differences concrete. These contrasts demonstrate two things: 1) the differences between God's way of living and the world's; 2) the way for nominal or young Christians to evaluate their walk with God. Every person's life will fall into one of the two categories. Personal reflection reveals if one is on the right road.

Jesus made frequent use of these contrasts. In the Sermon on the Mount, Jesus contrasted what others said with what He said (see Matt. 5:21,27,31,33,38,43). He indicated the differences between those trying to gain position or popularity by their religious activity and those whose actions were lived as unto Christ (see Matt. 6:1-18). Further, He warned

> One way of helping the mind grasp the things of God is to contrast God's will and the world's way.

of the folly of those who build their lives on human wisdom rather than God's (see Matt. 7:24-27).

The Epistles also contrast the two ways. Almost the entire New Testament contrasts sinfulness and holiness. But there are specific passages in which the writer spotlighted the differences between Christians and non-Christians. Passages like 1 Corinthians 6:9-11, Galatians 5:19-24, Ephesians 4:25–5:17, Colossians 3:5-17, 2 Timothy 3:1-17, and James 3:13-18 demonstrate the two ways of living. The contrasts often present extremes, characterizing unbelievers at their worst and believers at their best. Observing the extremes of non-Christian behavior warns us to do whatever we can to avoid them. On the other hand, observing the benefits of a Christian lifestyle encourages us to follow God's will.

PRINCIPLES OF CHRISTIAN GROWTH

Knowledge also includes principles of Christian growth. The starting point for all Christian growth is the conversion experience. The Holy Spirit convicts of sin. Recognizing their sin, persons under conviction about sin will cry for help. We say to God, "I will do anything to escape the sin which so destroys my life." God says: "You can't do anything, but I can. In fact, I already have. I have sent Jesus." God's mercy provides a way of escape. As the unbelieving sinner embraces God's Savior, the mind affirms two truths. One is the desire to change patterns of thinking about God, sin, and self. This is repentance. The other truth is to allow Jesus to reconstruct the life. While not all people recognize the full implications of accepting Jesus as Savior, in time these attitudes are clarified. The point is that repentance, faith, and embracing Jesus all make a person predisposed to a holy life as a believer.

> Repentance, faith, and embracing Jesus all make a person predisposed to a holy life as a believer.

Romans 6:1-14 clearly explains the experience of new life. Paul discussed the possibility that Christian people might entertain the idea of continuing to sin. Such a thought is unthinkable. Paul said, "By no means!" (v. 2)—it is also unnatural (see vv. 2-10). In refuting the idea, Paul took

Christians back to their conversion experience. We have been crucified with Christ, identifying with Him in death and resurrection. We have been spiritually baptized into Christ which means that God considers us one with Jesus. We share in all His experiences (vv. 4-11).

The shared experience with Christ includes both death and resurrection. In sharing His death, we died to sin as He did. We no longer live with sin as the ruling power in our lives. Recognizing that fact leads to an understanding of freedom from sin. As crucified people, we do not have to submit to sin's influence, power, or destiny. Sharing in Christ's experience also means participating in His resurrection. Just as He rose, we rose from our death to sin. We now have the power to live a new life with God as King. Sin no longer dominates our lives. God replaces Satan. Righteousness replaces sin. Eternal life replaces death. Our crucifixion with Christ at the conversion experience provides the basis of a new life–positionally and practically. Realizing the implications of that–the fact of our justification from sin–enables us to choose new directions for life.

Our crucifixion with Christ at the conversion experience provides the basis of a new life–positionally and practically.

CHOICES

People need more than knowledge. Good living depends on at least two things: accurate knowledge and proper choices. Accurate knowledge comes from understanding what the Bible teaches. Proper choices require a different type of skill. The world is full of people whose broken lives and failed relationships reveal the difficulty of making correct choices. The fact is that we will become what we *choose* to become. Choices make life what it is.

CHOICES PROMOTING HOLINESS

The Bible speaks powerfully on the subject of choices. There are myriads of both Old and New Testament commands. These commands relate to every conceivable aspect of life, always focusing on the principles that will bring happiness.

Every individual must decide whether or not to choose Christ.

CHOOSING SALVATION

Many factors lead a person to salvation. Jesus did His part in dying for sinners, and the Holy Spirit convicts and leads to confession of Christ. On the other hand, the Bible clearly teaches there is no salvation without personal choice. Every individual must decide whether or not to choose Christ. Predicting the coming day of the Lord, the prophet Joel prophesied a universal availability of salvation to those who would call on the Lord (see Joel 2:32). Both Peter and Paul quoted that Old Testament verse when they urged people to accept Christ (see Acts 2:21,40; Rom. 10:13-14). They affirmed that Jesus' death opened the day of salvation, but they realized that people had to choose to be a part of God's gift of grace. The most important choice of all is the choice to accept Christ. Until that decision is made, nothing else really matters. Once it is made, a new life begins.

CHOOSING TOTAL COMMITMENT

A second choice which promotes holiness is choosing complete dedication to Christ. Normally people will make this dedication at the time of conversion. But the testimony of some Christians reveals that for various reasons this choice was not clearly understood. Therefore, many completely dedicate themselves to God's will at some point after conversion.

The Old Testament anticipates a total involvement of a person's life with God. One example is Joshua, the great leader of Israel. He called the people to consider whom they would serve (see Josh. 24:15). In good leadership fashion he stated unequivocally his intention to serve the Lord. The New Testament continues the same theme. In Romans 12:1-2, Paul called his readers to "offer" themselves to the Lord as a "living sacrifice." The grammar of the verb "offer" reveals that Paul expected them to reach a climactic decision of commitment leading to a state of commitment. The mercies of God, described in Romans 1-11, lead us all to a total commitment to God.

The good gifts that accompany salvation come to those who have committed themselves completely to God. Complete dedication also brings the resources needed for a life of holiness. As God showers His good gifts on us, He leads us in ways that will develop holiness. Then as we develop holy lives, God blesses us with more of His presence.

CHOOSING HOLINESS DAY BY DAY

Day by day situations require decisions that will reinforce and encourage the life of holiness within. Sometimes we are called to react positively and Christlike to life's unpleasant or difficult events. At other times we have the responsibility of cultivating a lifestyle that reflects the glory of the holy God. Through both kinds of situations, God accomplishes His purpose of making us more Christlike.

Commands in Scripture are both direct and indirect. The indirect commands come from the logical applications of the didactic portions of the Bible. For example, Jesus told many parables. They present God's truth in realistic situations, and in every parable there is at least an implied action. Jesus expected His hearers to understand the point of the parable and act accordingly. Similarly, the passages with high christology call for a response of worship and/or thanksgiving for what God has done (see Eph. 1:3-14; Col. 1:9-20; Heb. 1:1-14, for example). There are implicit expectations of honoring Christ for who He is.

Parables present God's truth in realistic situations. Jesus expects us to understand the point and act accordingly.

On the other hand, some commands are directed toward specific growth patterns. They are relevant to the process of becoming holy (see Rom. 6:11-12). Two specific commands call for decisive action to overcome sin. First, "count yourselves dead to sin but alive to God in Christ Jesus" (v. 11). Then, "do not let sin reign in your mortal body so that you obey its evil desires" (v. 12). This last text is quite explicit in Greek. Literally it says, "Stop letting sin reign in your mortal bodies." Stopping implies the need for change from what characterizes life now to what life ought to be. Paul is equal-

CALLED TO BE HOLY

ly clear in other passages addressing the "old self/new self" issue. In Colossians 3:5 he says, "put to death ... whatever belongs to your earthly nature." *Putting to death* means "to keep these things from expressing themselves as they did before conversion." In verses 9 and 12, Paul used the imagery of changing clothes. He said, "You have taken off your old self" (v. 9). The metaphor is completed in verse 12 where he says, "cloth yourselves" with the good qualities that accompany Christian living.

Paul often contrasted sinful conduct and righteous living in what many have identified as "vice and virtue" lists. The sinful list contains idolatry and immorality. These were sins the Jews identified as the primary indicators of pagan religion. Most pagan religious practices worshiped false gods and engaged in religious sexual orgies. Paul also included sins representative of a loss of control (such as anger, wrath) and social abuses. Finally, there are sins of personal greed such as covetousness.

> **Holiness means walking with the Spirit of God so that the old ways of living are replaced by the fruit of the Spirit.**

By contrast, the new self is clothed with virtues that come from honoring the true God. They include self-control, social respect, and fairness. Holiness means walking with the Spirit of God so that the old ways of living are replaced by the fruit of the Spirit.

The vices and virtues remind us of the necessity of cooperating with God volitionally. Just as the Spirit of God does not override human personality and personal choices in bringing people to Christ, the Spirit of God will not violate human choices in life after conversion. While the Holy Spirit will urge one toward holiness as well as bring conviction about a wrong way of living, God will not force His way upon the believer. He does expect us to choose a new way of living based on new values and ambitions.

OPPOSITION TO PROPER CHOICES

Developing new patterns of life is never easy. While God expects us to make the correct choices, there is strong opposition to cultivating a life of holiness. The opposition comes both from outside and inside the believer.

EXTERNAL OPPOSITION

At conversion opposition to God's will intensifies. Knowledge is more difficult to attain, proper choices more difficult to make, and new habits more difficult to practice because of the spiritual warfare associated with the new life. The external opposition comes from the world, the flesh, and the enemy.

The Bible warns repeatedly about pressures generated from the world. The Greek word for *world* is *cosmos* and literally means "the earth." That is seldom its meaning in Scripture, however. Normally the word has a metaphorical meaning. It means "the world's systems." The world has a distinctive value system. It is a system of thought that is contrary to God and seeks to exclude God entirely. John warned about the world's power. He said: "Do not love the world or anything in the world. If anyone loves the world, the love of the Father is not in him" (1 John 2:15). James issued a similar warning: "You adulterous people, don't you know that friendship with the world is hatred toward God? Anyone who chooses to be a friend of the world becomes an enemy of God" (Jas. 4:4). These statements echo what both writers may have heard from Jesus Himself. Jesus knew His followers would be persecuted and warned them to expect it. He said: "If the world hates you, keep in mind that it hated me first. If you belonged to the world, it would love you as its own. As it is, you do not belong to the world, but I have chosen you out of the world. That is why the world hates you" (John 15:18-19).

The world's systems and institutions keep us from God. Again John warned, "The world and its desires pass away, but the man who does the will of God lives forever" (1 John 2:17). Our world does not promote holiness. Christians must make difficult choices to separate themselves from the world and to become like Christ.

Christians must make difficult choices to separate themselves from the world and to become like Christ.

The Bible also warns about the pressures of the flesh. The Greek word for *flesh* means "the meat of a person or an animal." Often the word is used literally, but it also has a metaphorical meaning with moral connotations. *The flesh* is the natural way of thinking and acting, unaided by the Holy Spirit. The primary difference between the world and the flesh is that the world is an environment, a system constructed by people. The flesh is the natural way these people view life. Like the world, the flesh is contrary to God. Paul warned about the dangers of following the flesh and the personal and corporate destruction it causes (see Gal. 5:19, literally the "works of the flesh"). Thinking in the flesh also brings "death" (Rom. 8:6). Such thinking is preoccupied with wrong desires (see v. 5), "is hostile to God," and "cannot please God" (vv. 7-8). This way of thinking creates value systems that are contrary to God's way (see 2 Cor. 5:16).

The task of becoming holy is to learn the way of the Spirit and allow the Spirit to overcome the way of the flesh.

The flesh is a characteristic way of viewing reality without considering God. It is the way unbelievers appraise things. The pressure from the flesh comes from the collective appraisals of all non-Christians, but it can also come from within the Christian. When Christians think and act like those without the Holy Spirit, they are living like the flesh (see 1 Cor. 3:1-3). The task of becoming holy is to learn the way of the Spirit and allow the Spirit to overcome the way of the flesh.

The Bible also describes the pressures that come from the enemy. Satan is called many things, but all point to him as a slanderer, deceiver, and promoter of evil. The devil opposes God and has done so from the beginning. John says of him: "He who does what is sinful is of the devil, because the devil has been sinning from the beginning. The reason the Son of God appeared was to destroy the devil's work" (1 John 3:8). Peter issued the same warning: "Your enemy the devil prowls around like a roaring lion looking for someone to devour" (1 Pet. 5:8). Again these warnings echo Jesus' own explanation of Satan's activity. When Peter questioned Jesus, Jesus said to Peter: "Get behind me, Satan! You are a stumbling block to me; you do not have in mind the things of God, but the things of men" (Matt. 16:23). Since Satan blinds people's eyes so they cannot understand the truth, he opposes all persons. The enemy seeks to counter the choices God's people should make.

These external influences make proper choices difficult to make. Some of the most pointed commands in Scripture warn about the world, the flesh, and the devil. In taking a strong stand for holiness and choosing what is best, the Christian can expect opposition. The world seeks to squeeze Christians into its mold, and that mold is far from holy.

In taking a strong stand for holiness and choosing what is best, the Christian can expect opposition.

INTERNAL OPPOSITION

Internal pressures also exert their influence. One task of believers is to possess a transformed mind that replaces the mind of the flesh with the mind of Christ. Progressively the mind is able to choose holiness because it progressively thinks in a holy way. There are other pressures that war against the Christian making proper choices. These are described in Scripture as lusts. In James 1:14 we read "each one is tempted when, by his own evil desire, he is dragged away and enticed." Temptation has both inside and outside aspects. Outside there is a lure, something that attracts our attention. Inside there is lust which moves toward the attraction on the outside. Temptation occurs in the interaction of these two.

The temptations basically fall into three major categories, although they manifest themselves in many specific ways. The three occur together in several passages and individually in many others. The concentrated passages are Genesis 3:6: "the woman saw that the fruit of the tree was good for food and pleasing to the eye, and also desirable for gaining wisdom"; Matthew 4:1-11 with Luke 4:1-13 and 1 John 2:16: "For everything in the world—the cravings of sinful man, the lust of his eyes and the boasting of what he has and does—comes not from the Father but from the world."

One area of temptation is passion (according to the references "good for food," "stones to become bread," and "cravings of sinful man"). All persons have difficulty learning to control their passions, but God gives power to control them. A second area of temptation is possessions (according to the references "pleasing to the eye," "all this I will give you," and "lust of his eyes"). There is a natural inclination to acquire things, and sometimes people acquire them in unethical, illegal, or unwise ways. The final area of temptation is position. The drive to be something and to be seen as someone causes us to seek prominent positions in our own ways rather than doing the will of God. The specific temptation may vary, but we can be sure that the world, the flesh, and the devil will take advantage of the desire to fulfill passions, acquire possessions, or occupy position.

This discussion reveals the difficulty of making proper choices. It is not easy to choose what is right. The naturally depraved mind, along with both external and internal opposition, means that the Christian must have a renewed mind and the resolve to choose correctly. Without proper choices, there will be no growth toward holiness.

POWER

The Holy Spirit knows our weaknesses and our temptations, but He also knows the way to victory.

Perhaps the most crucial issue confronting those who would change their lives is the ability to do it. Many times we know what is best and resolve to do it, but actually doing it is another matter. So what about people who cannot seem to accomplish what they choose? The Bible promises help for the weak-willed. The Holy Spirit is accessible to help in times of difficulty. In fact, one of the Holy Spirit's tasks is to bring the resources of God to us. He knows our weaknesses and our temptations, but He also knows the way to victory. The power for Christian living comes from the Holy Spirit.

The Spirit brings actual liberation from sin and death. At conversion we die to sin with Christ. The Bible says this is being "freed" from sin (Rom. 6:7). *Justification* is the word used in reference to a believer's standing with God. It points to a legal status but does not address the experience of sinning. Because of our death with Christ, we are declared free from sin. However, being declared free is not the same as experiencing freedom. In Romans 8:2 there is a different word used which literally means "liberation." Paul explained that the "the law of the Spirit of life set me free from the law of sin and death." Here the word for *set free* is "liberates." It means "enjoying the actual experience of freedom." What Jesus accomplished on the cross and what we come to know at conversion is applied to us by the Holy Spirit.

Those who seek to cooperate with the Holy Spirit's work desire the things of the Spirit (see Rom. 8:5-8). The Holy Spirit works on the mind to value God's life. Our ambitions are what we desire, and the Holy Spirit enables us to desire the things of the Spirit. Thus the Spirit works in the entire salvation experience. Paul explained in Romans 8:9 that we "are controlled not by the sinful nature but by the Spirit, if the Spirit of God lives in you. And if anyone does not have the Spirit of Christ, he does not belong to Christ." There is no need for any second experience in life to bring the Holy Spirit. The Holy Spirit comes at conversion and immediately begins His work, urging the believer to higher things. This is why believers who sin experience a new kind of conviction. At conversion we become "wholeheartedly" obedient to God (Rom. 6:17). Frustration occurs when we act out of harmony with our hearts.

There is much confusion about the sanctifying work of the Holy Spirit. Some teach the necessity of a pentecostal experience to bring the sanctifying power of the Holy Spirit. Nothing in Scripture confirms this position. Further, no passage of Scripture suggests that the believer should seek an experience of any kind, much less a pentecostal experience. Finally, the Spirit's presence at Pentecost had nothing to do with overcoming sin and achieving holiness.

Being declared free is not the same as experiencing freedom.

Others explain the Spirit's sanctifying work as the "filling of the Spirit." Once again there is confusion. When the Greek words for *filling* occur in connection with the Holy Spirit, there is no clear passage associating filling with holiness. As used in Luke and Acts, they are never connected to holiness. Rather they explain the ability to minister effectively. The words *filling* and *Holy Spirit* also occur together in Ephesians 5:18, but again have no connection to personal holiness.

In Galatians 5:16-26, Paul described the Holy Spirit's work in the believer. He used three terms of the Spirit's presence. The first occurs in verse 16. The *New International Version* translates it "live," but the Greek is literally "walk around" *(peripateo)*. This translation accurately expresses the idea. The believer is to conduct all of life in the sphere of the Spirit. The second verb occurs in verse 18. The NIV correctly translates it as "led." If the Holy Spirit leads believers, they are not under law. The Holy Spirit brings freedom from the law, giving internal standards rather than external and bringing God's power rather than self-effort. The final verb is "keep in step with the Spirit" (v. 25); in Greek the word is *stoicheo*. This rare word means "to place our feet in the place the Spirit leads." It was used of the military who marched "in step."

The Holy Spirit brings freedom from the law, giving internal standards rather than external and bringing God's power rather than self-effort.

All the verbs contribute to a proper understanding of the Holy Spirit's role. We are to invite the Holy Spirit to be present in every aspect of life. We are to follow the Holy Spirit as He leads us. More precisely, we must do exactly what the Holy Spirit commands, "putting our feet" where the Spirit "puts His." When this happens the believer will be characterized by the fruit of the Spirit (see Gal. 5:22-23) and will not accomplish the works of the flesh (see vv. 17,19-21).

The believer's primary concern is how to walk with the Spirit. The focus in Christian living is always obedience to Christ. The Holy Spirit empowers those who follow Christ consistently. Further, the more consistently we are in doing the will of God, the more available are the Spirit's resources.

As Christians focus on doing the will of God, the Holy Spirit's power comes to them. The Spirit renews the mind, applies the power of Christ, and leads in victory.

One of the learned skills of walking with the Spirit is discerning the balance between self-effort and appropriating God's power to avoid extremes. Some people approach life assuming they must do everything by self will. They treat God as a coach who stands on the sidelines and watches them play the game. Others approach life passively. They assume that Jesus should live through them, and they exert no self effort toward holiness. Usually they are easily frustrated because they do not experience the victory they expect. If it is up to Jesus or the Spirit, why aren't they perfect immediately? Neither approach is biblical.

Victory over sin comes in cooperation with the Holy Spirit. God generally does not do what we make no attempt to do. Part of correct choosing is exerting the effort to accomplish the choice made. On the other hand, even young Christians soon learn they cannot handle spiritual battles on their own strength. Satan's power is simply too great. Without the Holy Spirit's help, there is no victory. A serious choice to be holy means a sincere effort to do God's will. All the while there is a spirit of dependence and trust that the Holy Spirit will empower us to accomplish far more than we can on our own. Throughout Scripture, God accomplished His work through human effort. The principle also applies to the effort toward personal holiness.

A serious choice to be holy means a sincere effort to do God's will.

In the New Testament the Holy Spirit is contrasted with law. Since the Spirit brings power to the believer's life, it stands to reason that the law weakens us. The New Testament teaches uniformly that Christians no longer live under the law. The Gospels and the Epistles warn us about living under the law.

The apostle Paul wrote directly to the point. It was difficult for the Jewish Pharisee to leave the law. But when writing to the church at Colosse, Paul affirmed that "when you were dead in your sins and in the uncircumcision of your sinful nature, God made you alive with Christ. He forgave us all our sins, having canceled the written code, with its regulations, that was against us and that stood opposed to us; he took it away, nailing it to the cross" (Col. 2:13-14).

We are under grace, not law. While the law does have value as a *revelation* of God's character and His expectations, it has no value in *regulating* the Christian life. The attempt to live by any law, including the Ten Commandments, brings frustration and impotence. The power the law *seems* to encourage is *willpower*. The law is external, imposing itself on us and calling for a total obedience or else. The Jews of Paul's day believed their spiritual power resulted from keeping the law. But the only power they possessed was their own. In contrast, "if you are led by the Spirit, you are not under law" (Gal. 5:18). The power the Spirit brings is *God-power*.

We are under grace, not law.

We all want to live powerful lives. If we wish to have power, we must walk with the Holy Spirit. He freely brings God's power into our feeble lives, allowing us to accomplish everything God wills for us. Without the Holy Spirit we are left to our own strength and are hopeless. With God's powerful presence in our lives, we triumph in His strength.

CONCLUSION

Three essential ingredients promote growth. Without knowledge, proper choices, and the power of the Holy Spirit, Christians cannot grow. The church is responsible to teach the things of God in a steady diet of truth. The church must exhort believers to make good choices. And Christians must learn to walk in the power of the Holy Spirit. In short, all three efforts are necessary if Christians are to mature and be successful in the journey to holiness.

Complete Holiness

CHAPTER 6

REACHING THE GOAL

A very dramatic story occurred during the 1992 Olympics. The 400-meter race pitted some of the best athletes of the world in competition. A favorite was Derrick Redmond, a runner from Great Britain. Years of training, practice, mental preparation, and competition led him to this point in time. Like a finely tuned engine he lined up for his greatest race. He made a good start and ran exactly as he planned. In the last turn, he knew he had a chance.

Then the worst of fears was realized. Beginning the stretch toward the finish line, he pulled a hamstring muscle and fell helplessly to the track. Derrick tried repeatedly to stand and finish the race—but to no avail. No doubt his emotional pain was greater than the physical as he watched the remaining runners streak by and cross the finish line. But Derrick was a champion. Refusing to give up, he kept trying to walk and then crawl to the finish line. Knowing his chance for a medal was gone, he still struggled to finish the race.

One man in the crowd sensed the moment. He rushed to the rail, pushed away the guards, and ran to the hurting runner. The crowd's attention turned to the stranger. He knelt down, lifted the runner, and supported him as together they hobbled to the finish line. The crowd cheered for this great demonstration of spirit. Before Derrick crossed the finish line, the media researchers had identified the stranger from the crowd. It was Derrick's father.

This true story has many applications to our study of holiness. Christians run the race of their lives looking toward

Christians run the race of their lives looking toward the finish line when they will see Christ.

the finish line when they will see Christ. They know they will finish, but sometimes the race brings unexpected circumstances. Because of the weaknesses of the flesh, we also know we need help. There are times when everyone does. Like Derrick's father, God provides the needed help to allow us to finish the course. Our Heavenly Father guarantees we will finish.

In this chapter we will discuss the helps God provides to keep us moving toward holiness. We will also discuss, in more detail than previously discussed, the final stage of perfection. We have presented the definition of holiness and the way of transformation so that we can become progressively holy in this life. Now our thoughts turn to the future. Who is there to help, and what will the end be?

HELPS FOR GROWING IN HOLINESS

Transformation from the old person's lifestyle to the new person's lifestyle requires personal resolve and commitment.

The transformation from the old person's lifestyle to the new person's lifestyle requires personal resolve and commitment. Although it is the most rewarding life we can ever experience, living the new life can feel quite lonely and sometimes fearful. Success results from taking advantage of the following helps that God provides to help us grow.

THE BIBLE AND NATURAL REVELATION

The Bible is by far the most important tool God has provided for us. The Bible was inspired by God. Also, it is God's most effective means of promoting His interests in the world. God reveals Himself in the Bible in two primary ways: natural and special revelation.

God reveals Himself through natural channels, also called general revelation. This includes creation, human conscience and intellect, and history.

The creation is His handiwork. It demonstrates God's presence and greatness much like a painting points to the quality of the painter. In studying creation one gets a sense of order and power, good and evil, and the possibility of new life. There are, however, serious limitations to the knowledge gained about God through creation. Those who prefer to derive their theology only from nature will likely be misguided. Nature simply is not clear enough.

We can learn truths about God from studying human conscience and intellect. God created us in His image. Even with the fall into sin and the resulting depravity, we all have a vestige of God's image in us. Paul spoke of this as the law of God "written on their hearts" (Rom. 2:14-15). People discover universal moral laws. As we collectively study the nature of God, it is possible to arrive at some fairly accurate conclusions about what God must be like. We assume He is a God of love, justice, power, mercy, and personality. These all come from our understanding of human characteristics and thought patterns. Since we are created in God's image, there is a sense in which we can derive some knowledge of God from human reason. Even so, human reason alone will never construct an accurate picture of God. Left to ourselves, we will never know how to live for Him.

Human reason alone will never construct an accurate picture of God.

History is a way of understanding God. God works in and through the affairs of life. Not only does God work through them, but also He orchestrates them in His own way (see Acts 17:26-27). A study of history should help us to find God because He is always there. Yet history is too clouded with sin to derive a clear theology of God.

These three examples of natural revelation help explain human ideas about God's expectations. But the conclusions can be seriously misguided because natural revelation is a partial disclosure of God to people whose minds are blinded to the truth. We can learn much about God through human reason and social consciousness. Yet, we cannot know everything and what we learn may be distorted. Natural revelation is inadequate.

God also reveals Himself through special revelation. In inspiring the Bible, God devised a way to communicate His truth to us accurately and relevantly. He used human experience, observations, ideas, and situations as the vehicles through which divine truth came. The contexts of the various portions of the Bible make the truth alive to people of all ages, especially those who live in situations similar to those the Bible addressed originally. The Bible corrects natural revelation and extends it to truths not understandable through nature.

The Bible is our guide. At the end of his life, the apostle Paul explained this to Timothy. Looking back over the years of his own experience and looking ahead to the responsibilities Timothy would assume, Paul wrote, "All Scripture is God-breathed and is useful for teaching, rebuking, correcting and training in righteousness, so that the man of God may be thoroughly equipped for every good work" (2 Tim. 3:16-17).

A commitment to Christ and to holiness means a commitment to the Bible as the Word of God and the only sufficient guide for life and godliness. Christians throughout the centuries have found the more time they spend with the Bible the better they live their lives. They have studied it seriously and meditated on it personally. God speaks through the words of Scripture, and the Holy Spirit uses them to provide spiritual stability and to develop Christian character. Yet the Bible is not the end in itself. It bears witness to Jesus as Lord. It explains how we come to know Jesus and how we can be true to Him on earth.

> **A commitment to Christ and to holiness means a commitment to the Bible as the Word of God and the only sufficient guide for life and godliness.**

PRAYER

The second help in attaining a holy life is prayer. The example of Scripture and the testimony of Christians through the centuries confirm prayer as a means of grace. In prayer we develop our relationship with God, we learn His expectations for our lives, and we receive power and direction. Serious Christians devote themselves to prayer.

The Bible records many types of prayers. Some prayers are for praise, appreciating God for who He is and what He has done (see Eph. 1:3-14). Other prayers consist of petition, bringing to God the concerns of life, expecting Him to understand and respond.

Christians prayed in times of political oppression (see Acts 4:23-31), to understand God's will for their lives (see Acts 10:9-23), and for safety and deliverance (see Acts 12:5). Scripture also teaches to pray for wisdom (see Jas. 1:5) and for God's provision for our needs (see Matt. 5:3-12). We are to bathe all of life in prayer (see Phil. 4:6-7; Jas. 5:13-18).

Paul prayed for the holiness of the church at Ephesus: "I pray also that the eyes of your heart may be enlightened in order that you may know the hope to which he has called you, the riches of his glorious inheritance in the saints, and his incomparably great power for us who believe" (Eph. 1:18-19). This prayer specifically asks for the "eyes of your heart" to "be enlightened." To have the heart enlightened is to pray for illumination of the mind–knowledge–and the heart–choices–so that God can reveal Himself. The goal of all holiness is to be like Christ in the restored image of God. Holiness comes, in part, from an effective prayer life and, conversely, holiness promotes effective prayer (see Jas. 5:16).

To have the heart enlightened is to pray for illumination of the mind–knowledge–and the heart–choices–so that God can reveal Himself.

PERSONAL LEARNING ACTIVITY

**How is the Holy Spirit working in your life?
If you are aware that He is working
in your life, list the ways.**

_____

_____

**Consider keeping a prayer journal (if you don't
already) to record God's work in your life.**

CHRISTIAN COMMUNITY

Christian community is essential for individual Christian growth in holiness.

Another help in achieving holiness is Christian community. Christian community occurs through the church. This is the Christian's primary environment for spiritual growth. Those who have attempted to grow in Christ without the church have found serious limitations. The church is the visible body of Christ. Theologians have correctly affirmed that when people are placed into the spiritual body of Christ at conversion, they should express that immediately by becoming a part of the visible body of Christ through baptism and church membership. In the church Christians share their spiritual gifts, express mutual concerns and care for one another, and multiply their witness to the world around them. Christian community is essential for individual Christian growth in holiness.

Paul addressed this specifically in Ephesians. He wrote, "It was he who gave some to be apostles, some to be prophets, some to be evangelists, and some to be pastors and teachers, to prepare God's people for works of service, so that the body of Christ may be built up until we all reach unity in the faith and in the knowledge of the Son of God and become mature, attaining to the whole measure of the fullness of Christ" (Eph. 4:11-13). Christian leaders build up God's people for works of service. Service enables the church to grow in unity and knowledge. The final stage is "attaining to the whole measure of the fullness of Christ." The various spiritual gifts build up the whole until each Christian arrives at the goal. As Christians grow together and relate honestly with one another, they "grow up into him who is the Head" (Eph. 4:15). Such growth is a group process with a clear goal to be like Christ.

There are other advantages to being in the church. Using the body metaphor, Paul explained that everyone has an important place in the fellowship (see 1 Cor. 12:14-26). When the church functions as it should, there is honor and loving concern for all. Everyone can grow to full maturity. There are always Christians who do not represent the body of Christ as we hope they would. Rather than scorning them, we should provide special care and nurture for them (see v. 23). The church also provides an environment to smooth out the rough edges. In community we care about our commitment to God and about our relationships with others in the church. That means both the individual and the group devote time and energy to heal one another. Christians should be sympathetic to others' weaknesses as well as committed to the corporate growth of the church.

Paul also explained that Christians cannot understand the love of Christ as they should without other Christians. In Ephesians 3:17-19, he described growth in love. There are three stages of experiencing the love of Christ. First, Christians are "rooted and established in love." The salvation experience is the greatest expression of the love of God. Second, based on that foundation, Christians should grow together in their understanding of love. As we see the love of God expressed to others and lived through others, we gain more insight into the magnificent breadth of God's love ("how wide and long and high and deep," 3:18). Third, as church members interrelate, understanding and appreciating what God has done in one another, they come to know the fullness of His love. We cannot know everything by ourselves. Further, we cannot grow into holiness by ourselves. Mutual relationships promote growth (v. 23).

As we see the love of God expressed to others and lived through others, we gain more insight into the magnificent breadth of God's love.

PERSONAL LEARNING ACTIVITY

List the ways your church is currently helping you to grow in Christ.

_____

_____

_____

113

List the ways you are giving back to your church and helping others to grow in Christ.

_____

_____

CHRISTIAN SERVICE

Ministry builds holiness by causing us to search our motives, message, and methods of service.

Ministry builds character and holiness. It builds holiness in two ways. First, life changes as we confront difficult situations. We examine ourselves, especially our abilities, and we learn to trust in Christ for power. The dynamics of serving provide an environment that purifies our lives. Second, ministry builds holiness by causing us to search our motives, message, and methods of service. Spiritual work requires the power of the Holy Spirit. The Holy Spirit works best through obedient people who are fully seeking to know Christ. Regular service, therefore, causes us to examine our lives. Ministry takes us to the spiritual battleground where we war against powers stronger than human beings (see Eph. 6:10-18). Victory comes only from the power of Christ, and there is a correlation between victory in Christ and personal holiness. Christians grow through service. If we desire to be holy, we must serve Christ.

PERSONAL LEARNING ACTIVITY

What ministries do you offer for Christ?

_____

How is this ministry a blessing to others?

_____

How is this ministry helping you in your quest for holiness?

_____

114

SUFFERING

A fourth help toward achieving holiness is suffering. Suffering is the only help that appears to be negative. No one chooses to suffer. Yet we know of both scriptural and personal examples of times when God used suffering to bring Christians closer to Himself. God does not need suffering to accomplish His purposes, and He did not ordain it. If we did not live in a fallen world, there would be no sickness, sorrow, or suffering. But the Bible teaches that God works through human suffering. Whether physical, emotional, mental, relational, or spiritual suffering, God does something special in those who trust Him and endure it.

Romans 5:3-5 describes a growth process beginning with trials, an externally induced cause of suffering: "we know that suffering produces perseverance; perseverance, character; and character, hope. And hope does not disappoint us, because God has poured out his love into our hearts by the Holy Spirit, whom he has given us." In this text, character is the equivalent of holiness. It is a permanent quality in the believer. James reminded his readers of the same benefit. In James 1:3-4 he said: "You know that the testing of your faith develops perseverance. Perseverance must finish its work so that you may be mature and complete, not lacking anything." Many consider times of trial to be periods of God's inactivity. Nothing could be further from the truth. These texts reveal that the activity of God is very positive and active. God uses difficult times to move us toward holiness.

God uses difficult times to move us toward holiness.

Trials also equip us to minister more effectively. Paul explained in 2 Corinthians 1:3-5 that God comforts His people so that they can comfort others with the same comfort He provides. God's comfort comes to us through the lens of Christ's suffering. Jesus Himself endured suffering leading up to His death. The writer of Hebrews stated, "In bringing many sons to glory, it was fitting that God, for whom and through whom everything exists, should make the author of their salvation perfect through suffering"

(2:10). Suffering promotes holiness and builds character. Effective ministry is a result.

The suffering of Jesus enables Him to help others endure their own suffering. Hebrews says, "Because he himself suffered when he was tempted, he is able to help those who are being tempted" (2:18). The experiences endured by Jesus provided a greater sympathy with those who face similar situations. Further, Hebrews identifies preparation for the ministry of the cross with suffering. Jesus learned obedience through suffering, and with obedience He accomplished His sacrificial death for us (see Heb. 5:7-9). Suffering and obedience uniquely prepare us for service to God.

In suffering we see the remarkable grace of God.

In suffering we see the remarkable grace of God. God uses situations that arise out of a sinful environment to accomplish His purposes for the believer. When Satan throws his best, God triumphs by using the situation developmentally in the life of His people.

PERSONAL LEARNING ACTIVITY

In a few sentences, describe an experience with suffering that has helped in your growth as a Christian and your quest for holiness.

_____

_____

_____

THE COMPLETION OF HOLINESS

We have discussed the meaning of holiness, the process of becoming holy, and the helps that bring us to a holy state. One subject remains: the completion of holiness. As we have seen, holiness may be divided into three stages: positional holiness, progressive holiness, and perfect holiness. At conversion the believer is positionally holy, and at that time there is a guarantee that holiness will be completed in the believer's life. It is helpful to see what that means for the believer.

Sanctification and glorification overlap at certain points. Glorification is the doctrine that describes the ultimate goal of all of salvation. In His high priestly prayer, John 17, Jesus prayed for His glorification. There He prayed that God would "glorify me in your presence with the glory I had with you before the world began" (v. 5). Jesus anxiously awaited the time when He would be restored to His true glory. His glorification is seen after the resurrection when He appeared in a new state with a glorified body. The believers' hope is that we will be like Jesus.

GUARANTEE OF COMPLETE HOLINESS

The Bible clearly teaches that all who accept Christ will be like Him. The guarantee of ultimate salvation and of the believer's holiness does not depend on the believer. Just as God accepts the sinner who trusts in Christ, God perfects those who are in Christ. Many passages affirm this truth.

Our conformity to Christ was the purpose of salvation. Romans 8:29-30 describes the entire process as God sees it: "For those God foreknew he also predestined to be conformed to the likeness of his Son, that he might be the first-born among many brothers. And those he predestined, he also called; those he called, he also justified; those he justified, he also glorified." The two verses in this passage take two slightly different approaches to the same end. Verse 29 links foreknowledge and predestination. Predestination means to draw the horizons of life in advance. Using this definition, God drew the boundaries of our lives as believers before we lived them. Every believer can expect to be like Christ. That is God's plan and His choice. Complete holiness is to be re-created in the image of Christ. Verse 30 views the same end using different words. There is an unbreakable

Complete holiness is to be re-created in the image of Christ.

chain of God's choices for us and His actions toward us. Once one is predestined, glorification is guaranteed.

The Holy Spirit is God's seal upon us and guarantees that we will arrive at our intended destination.

As proof of this, Paul explained that God gave us the Holy Spirit to assure us of future glory. In Ephesians 1:13-14 Paul used two metaphors of the Spirit. The first occurs in verse 13: "And you also were included in Christ when you heard the word of truth, the gospel of your salvation. Having believed, you were marked in him with a seal, the promised Holy Spirit." The seal was a personalized guarantee of authenticity and protection. Frequently, it was used in the postal system of the day. When a person of influence posted a letter, the letter was sealed in wax. The process included melting hot wax on the flap of the letter. Then a personalized, engraved ring was pressed into the wax. The seal would not be broken until the letter reached its recipient. Paul's use of the metaphor describes the Holy Spirit as God's seal upon us. The seal guarantees we will arrive at our intended destination.

The second metaphor comes from the economic practices of the day. Then, as now, often someone would purchase major items in stages. For example, a down payment to be followed by the complete price amount. Applying the terminology to Christians, Paul explained that the Holy Spirit is God's down payment, "who is a deposit guaranteeing our inheritance until the redemption of those who are God's possession" (v. 14). The verse indicates that God intends to complete the process He began. The Holy Spirit within believers guarantees that God will bring us to glory.

Paul also associated this with our identification with Jesus' death. In Romans 6:5 Paul stated, "If we have been united with him like this in his death, we will certainly also be united with him in his resurrection." The death of Christ means we will share in the resurrection. Sin will not have final power over us, but rather we will be able to live someday without the limitations imposed by sin (see v. 14).

The guarantee of glory is associated with the love of Christ, best shown in His death. Paul wrote one of the most loved of all passages in this light. He said, "For I am convinced that neither death nor life, neither angels nor demons, neither the present nor the future, nor any powers, neither height nor depth, nor anything else in all creation, will be able to separate us from the love of God that is in Christ Jesus our Lord" (Rom. 8:38-39). Nothing can keep a believer from receiving everything God planned.

Nothing can keep a believer from receiving everything God planned.

MORAL PERFECTION

The most obvious aspect of complete holiness is moral perfection. We identify holiness with living morally blameless lives. Colossians 1:22 promises this for the believer: "he has reconciled you by Christ's physical body through death to present you holy in his sight, without blemish and free from accusation." Paul explained holiness as "without blemish" and "free from accusation." Without blemish comes from the picture of something created without flaw. Flawless means perfect. Free from accusation means that no one can indict us for any activity. No one can fault a believer for anything he or she has done. Together these speak powerfully to complete holiness. They take us to a future time when character and activity will be completely holy. The only way God can do this is to forgive our sins through what Jesus has done. Other New Testament texts confirm that the believer will be "without blemish" (Eph. 1:4; Jude 24) and "without accusation" (1 Cor. 1:8; Phil. 1:9-11).

Moral perfection comes because we have complete and full knowledge. Earlier we discussed the necessity of being transformed by having a renewed mind (see Rom. 12:2). Knowledge is one of the essential aspects of personal growth. The logical end is that we will someday know completely and be completely transformed. Paul taught that a time will come when believers have complete knowledge. He said in 1 Corinthians 13:12: "Now we see but a poor reflection as in a mirror; then we shall see face to face. Now I know in part;

then I shall know fully, even as I am fully known." The apostle John expressed the same truth: "Dear friends, now we are children of God, and what we will be has not yet been made known. But we know that when he appears, we shall be like him, for we shall see him as he is" (1 John 3:2). This refers to moral perfection such as Christ possessed. John explained this as a motivation to purity. In verse 3 he said, "Everyone who has this hope in him purifies himself, just as he is pure." Clearly the likeness to Christ brings purity, "just as he is pure."

Complete purity is our ultimate condition. Holiness was lost in the garden of Eden. The purpose of Jesus' death was to provide holiness for those who had lost it, and God promises holiness to all who accept Christ. The moral perfection God intends will come—but it will come in the future.

Completed sanctification comes at death when we know fully, see Christ perfectly, and stand without accusation.

Completed sanctification comes at death when we know fully, see Christ perfectly, and stand without accusation. There is no sinless perfection in this life. In fact, John warns that those who believe they can achieve a condition of sinlessness are in error. He writes in 1 John 1:8: "If we claim to be without sin, we deceive ourselves and the truth is not in us." Something must occur to bring us to a state of perfect holiness. At death God brings us to perfection.

BODILY PERFECTION

There is a close connection between the body and the soul. We are shaped in large part by the attributes of our bodies. Much of how we think of ourselves and how we act toward others is a reaction to natural or physical characteristics. We cannot conceive of ourselves without a body.

The close connection between body and soul impacts us spiritually. The vehicle through which temptations come is the body. The body allows us to visualize the object of temptation and then the body moves toward attaining those temporary satisfactions. However, progressive holiness occurs in the body. For that reason Paul wrote that we are to commit our bodies to the Lord "as living sacrifices" (Rom. 12:1). We are to keep sin from reigning in our mortal bodies and to present our bodies "as instruments of righteousness" rather than unrighteousness (Rom. 6:12-13). In 1 Corinthians 6:13 Paul reminded us that "the body is not meant for sexual immorality, but for the Lord, and the Lord for the body." These references indicate that the body is to become holy as well as the soul. Deeds done in the body have eternal significance since the body can be the vehicle for accomplishing God's will. Paul said, "For we must all appear before the judgment seat of Christ, that each one may receive what is due him for the things done while in the body, whether good or bad" (2 Cor. 5:10).

God expects sanctification in the body. In a real sense, if it does not take place there, it will not take place. There is a deep theological reason for the discussion about the body. It may be illustrated from the use of the body in sexual relationships. When God created us, He gave us the beauty and responsibility of reproduction. Immediately upon creation God established the foundation for marriage. He said that man and woman were to leave father and mother, cleave only to themselves, and become one flesh (see Gen. 2:24). From that point the Bible reveals God's plan that husband and wife are to be sexually faithful and monogamous. This is for human good, but Scripture also hints of a deeper reason. First Corinthians 6:13 warns about sexual immorality because the body is "for the Lord." According to 1 Corinthians 7:4, the body also belongs to the spouse while on earth in the relationship of marriage. However, in heaven there is no marriage or giving in marriage (see Matt. 22:30). Apparently, there will be no sexual relationships, since we will be like the angels, who do not reproduce.

Why, then, is there so much emphasis on the purity of the body? The bodily resurrection is an important tenet of orthodox Christianity, and Paul argued at great length that

Deeds done in the body have eternal significance since the body can be the vehicle for accomplishing God's will.

What agreement is there between the temple of God and idols? For we are the temple of the living God. As God has said: "I will live with them and walk among them, and I will be their God, and they will be my people."
2 Corinthians 6:16

the body will be resurrected (see 1 Cor. 15:35-58). God created our bodies. They belong to Him, and at conversion they become His dwelling place (see 2 Cor. 6:16). In the resurrection they will belong to Him in a unique way. All of this suggests that God has a special interest in our bodies. Transformation of the body is an important part of His plan for redemption. As sin inhabits our bodies on earth, redemption will reverse that so that the body lives without sin.

Sanctification cannot be complete without it including our bodies. The Bible states that God will transform our bodies so that they will be perfect like the soul. Three primary Pauline passages speak of this. In Philippians 3:20-21, Paul said: "But our citizenship is in heaven. And we eagerly await a Savior from there, the Lord Jesus Christ, who, by the power that enables him to bring everything under his control, will transform our lowly bodies so that they will be like his glorious body." This text contributes two major truths. First, the body will be transformed to be like Jesus' body. We may correctly study the postresurrection passages in the Gospels to determine what our heavenly bodies will be like. They will be like Christ's body after His resurrection. Second, Jesus' power accomplishes this at the second coming. The completion of our holiness cannot be achieved progressively. It comes climactically.

Paul further described the nature of the heavenly body. It is heavenly not earthly and, therefore, is suited to heaven (see 2 Cor. 5:1-5). Since only perfection exists in heaven, it stands to reason that the body will be perfect and perfectly suited to that environment. Further, it is a spiritually maintained body (see 1 Cor. 15:42-49). This contrasts with "flesh and blood," which leads us to suggest that life in heaven is maintained by spiritual energy rather than air, food, and sun. Somehow spiritual power replaces the blood so that no longer is life in the blood as it is on earth. While these passages teach us about the nature of the body, one verse explains the transformation that will take place. Paul stated,

"And just as we have borne the likeness of the earthly man, so shall we bear the likeness of the man from heaven" (1 Cor. 15:49). The "likeness of the man from heaven" alternately states the goal of being "in the image of our creator," the goal of holiness. The entire discussion of the eternal body relates to holiness. Without a transformation of the body, holiness is incomplete.

While we long for perfection since God has delivered us from sin, we will not achieve it until death. At that time we will have the moral perfection we all seek. Similarly, our physical bodies long for a complete redemption. There is restlessness of body just as there is of soul. Paul expressed this clearly in Romans 8:23: "Not only so, but we ourselves, who have the firstfruits of the Spirit, groan inwardly as we wait eagerly for our adoption as sons, the redemption of our bodies." Someday the body will not be the instrument of sin but of pure worship. Although our bodies on earth have limitations, someday these will be removed.

When God completes redemption with the resurrection from the dead, believers will be whole. Holiness will become a reality. Both the material and the immaterial human parts will be transformed into the image of Christ.

> **When God completes redemption with the resurrection from the dead, believers will be whole–and holiness a reality.**

PRACTICAL IMPLICATIONS

No discussion of holiness is complete without discussion of practical matters. While many of the subjects of the various chapters already lend themselves to practical applications, a section devoted to implementation may help to organize the thoughts presented. Balanced Christian living always grows out of proper theology. Consider these implications.

Holiness comes from knowing our destination. God saved us to bring us to the restored image of Christ, and He will accomplish that in us. Knowing that provides direction in life. No Christian should ignore the implications of holy living. Many self-actualization books encourage us to visualize what we would like to be, then live that out day by day. The advice pertains to the Christian life as well. We should meditate on what we will be, then seek day by day to live holy lives in accordance with that decision.

Holiness comes from accepting responsibility. Scripture affirms that it is the person who is transformed, and that transformation comes through personal choices. While everyone needs God's power to effect radical change in life, the direct commands of the Bible teach that the individual can, and must, choose to live for God.

Holiness comes from disciplined obedience. People err in assuming that some mystical experience will suddenly make them holy. Scripture does not support this idea. Another way is to hope that God will do it for us, but passive people do not just arrive at holiness. A third is the idea that there is no need to discipline life to achieve holiness. Christians testify that the single most important secret of success is to walk with Christ in an organized and disciplined way. Regular times of Bible study, prayer, worship, and ministry bring multiplied benefits over time. God's power comes to those who obey Christ.

Holiness comes from viewing the destination. Many Christians measure their holiness by how far they have come since conversion. Certainly looking back is helpful. We derive encouragement from observing how much our lives have changed. But there are also dangers associated with looking back. For Christians the goal is to be like Christ. For many the goal is to be different from the world. They rejoice as they look back over their shoulders and view the distance between them and the non-Christian world. But separation is never the ultimate goal—Christlikeness is. Using any other benchmark for success causes us to measure ourselves by external and temporal reference points which foster pride and divide Christians.

Separation is never the ultimate goal— Christlikeness is.

Holiness comes from making good choices. Greater knowledge brings greater responsibility, but it does not necessarily bring a better way of life. Wishing to live in the manner we know is best begins a process but wishing alone does not help. In fact, many people experience frustrated lives because they do not achieve their spiritual hopes or wishes. The difference between what we know and how we live causes frustration.

The commands in God's Word call for a response. The emphasis in Scripture is on choosing. The Bible acknowledges that people choose good or evil, and it encourages us to make good choices. Only good choices bring holiness.

CONCLUSION

A study such as this forces us to fall on our faces in humility and confession. We can always grow in our Christian lives. In the days ahead, may we be found faithful to our high and holy calling. We must live every day fully trusting in God's love, forgiveness, strength, and purposes for us. We are new people, and we have new power and new potential. May we develop to our full potential "in Christ."

Finally, we should have a deep confidence. We know that God will complete what He started. The moment of conversion we were assured of complete victory. Our confidence is that God will guide us to glory, and there we will fellowship with Him in a completely holy state—soul and body. Our confidence in these brings hope day by day. Even if life seems overwhelming and the world, the flesh, and the enemy overbearing, God will give us the victory. Holiness is becoming like Jesus Christ day by day, step by step, relationship by relationship, and victory after victory. We are victors not victims since we know that "he who began a good work in you will carry it on to completion until the day of Christ Jesus" (Phil. 1:6). May our Lord make it so!

Holiness is becoming like Jesus Christ day by day, step by step, relationship by relationship, and victory after victory.

Holiness comes from making good choices. This study challenges us to make right choices that we might become holy. List three things that you will begin to do immediately in your quest for holiness.

_____

_____

_____

_____